.

REACHABLE:

7 KEYS TO LOVING, MENTORING, AND LEADING THE CHURCH OF THE NEXT GENERATION

DR. JEFFERY D. SKINNER

Trilogy Christian Publishers

A Wholly Owned Subsidiary of Trinity Broadcasting Network

2442 Michelle Drive

Tustin, CA 92780

For information, address Trilogy Christian Publishing

Rights Department, 2442 Michelle Drive, Tustin, Ca 92780.

Trilogy Christian Publishing/ TBN and colophon are trademarks of

Trinity Broadcasting Network.

For information about special discounts for bulk purchases, please contact Trilogy Christian Publishing.

Trilogy Disclaimer: The views and content expressed in this book are those of the author and may not necessarily reflect the views and doctrine of Trilogy Christian Publishing or the Trinity Broadcasting Network.

9798327121041

Library of Congress Cataloging-in-Publication Data is available.

ISBN 979-8-327112-104-1

ISBN 979-8-89041-829-6 (ebook)

Dedication

I dedicate this book to my grandfather and the small-town Alabama church. Their unwavering love and influence greatly impacted my faith journey. They demonstrated incredible patience, embracing a hyperactive, self-dressed six-year-old, and took deliberate steps to nurture my Christian identity. Their guidance laid the foundation upon which many others would build over the course of decades. I express my heartfelt gratitude for not only showing me the path alongside Jesus but also for being my steadfast companions on this spiritual journey.

Foreword

Recently I received a message from a pastor in his 50s, who told me that he remembered me coming and singing at his church when he was a little boy. It was that note, and others like it, that are continual reminders that I am no longer a member of the younger crowd—neither in society nor in the church. Time marches on, and everything is changing, often at a speed beyond our own imagination or ability to absorb. At the same time, we serve a transcendent God who is calling us into a future that is already being prepared for us. Therefore, no matter our age nor our station in life, we can be confident of the journey that we are to take with the Lord.

For those who are engaged in ministry, we embrace the journey with our Lord and are sustained and made confident in Him. We do not need to live in fear of the current state of affairs, nor of society, for God is at work. Dr. Skinner has created this beautiful and approachable work that invites us to leave our fears behind and delve into authentic relationship with those of a younger generation. The world would like to frighten us into believing that there is no hope for the future of the church, but if we truly believe that the church is the bride of Christ, then we cannot succumb to that fear.

Each chapter of this work is carefully crafted but also accessible, giving us tools to minister in changing times. We are challenged to embrace authenticity and relationship across the generations. Just like a family, younger generations are hungry for "moms," "dads," "grandmas," and "grandpas" that they may be able to find in the church. In a world filled with technology, the value of a meal at a home, followed by fellowship and conversation, may sound simple, and yet it becomes thoroughly engaging. You will leave this text challenged to consider the ways in which you may become more intentional in opening your heart and life to new relationships.

Foundational to all the work that we do within the church is prayer. Years ago, we were working with a strategist regarding our work and ministry and we discussed the need to make prayer an emphasis. I remember him responding, "Well, that's a given." The reality is that it is not a given, and not enough ministries deliberatively carve out space for prayer. It is, as Dr. Skinner reminds us, in the "thin space," where heaven and earth come together through participation in the divine in prayer that God's transformative power is at work. With that experience we can move into action, participating in covenant, and then empowered to move into the unknown of our current world and culture. That's why we don't need to be afraid of ministry in today's world.

If you are wondering whether you can continue to minister in this day and age, I encourage you to keep reading. The seven keys found in this text will inspire you, and you will discover that they are readily accessible. Dig in, read these encouraging words and roadmap, but then be ready to take action. First, in your own discipleship journey, then with your congregation, and finally with those you will encounter along the way.

Carla Sunberg
Kansas City
December 2023

Preface

Welcome to a journey unlike any other, an expedition into the profound depths of discipleship across generations. This is not your typical "how-to" guide, nor will you find a list of five easy steps to guaranteed success. Instead, prepare to embark on an exploration that will engage your heart, stimulate your mind, and nourish your soul.

Consider this book an invitation, one best accepted with a companion by your side, ideally from the next generation. Within these pages, you'll discover remarkable stories of individuals who, through their unwavering faith, have left an indelible mark on the world. But let me clarify: our purpose here is not solely to marvel at these inspiring examples. No, it goes much deeper than that.

This journey begins in the sacred sanctuary of self-reflection—a prayer closet, if you will. Here, we urge you to invite God to reveal your own blind spots, the areas of your heart and life that may unwittingly hinder others from finding their way into the kingdom of God. It's astonishing how the enemy can twist our own hurts and disappointments into barriers for those seeking the light of Christ.

Fear not, for this introspection is not meant to discourage but to prepare you for the path ahead. In this quiet space, implore God to heal your hurts and redeem your pain. Trust that this healing process is but the initial stage of your expedition.

Next, let your prayers seek guidance from the Lord. Implore the Holy Spirit for wisdom, not as a formula but as a humble request for direction. Pose the question to Jesus Himself: "How can I, with my unique experiences, serve as a vessel of grace for the next generation in ways only You can orchestrate?"

Know that your journey will be as distinctive as your own fingerprint, a path marked by God's hands as He is gently guiding your steps. As you embark on this adventure, may you do so with the blessings of Godspeed, fortified by the unwavering assurance of His presence.

Yours in faith and fellowship,
Dr. Jeffery D. Skinner

Acknowledgments

I extend my heartfelt thanks to my wife, Lisa, for her unwavering support throughout our thirty-one years of marriage and her dedication to proofreading and providing valuable content suggestions that have significantly improved this book. I'm grateful for her patience as I navigate the peaks and valleys of faith.

I also want to express my gratitude to my two children, Blaine and Hayden, who have taught me the significance of listening and learning from the next generations. Their insights have enriched my understanding. I love you to the moon!

Lastly, I extend my thanks to the remarkable team at the I Have a Message foundation, who have joined me on this journey, offering invaluable coaching and guidance throughout the book's creation.

Introduction

Our Motive for Mission

"The deepest motive for mission is simply the desire to be with Jesus where he is, on the frontier between the reign of God and the usurped dominion of the devil."[1]

Throughout my formative years, I had the privilege of growing up in a church that left an indelible mark on my heart and soul. Every Sunday, my sister and I would eagerly await the arrival of the Snoopy church bus, driven by our neighborhood's beloved Dairy Fresh milkman, ready to whisk us away to church. Once on board, Ms. Elaine, the bus driver's helper, would distribute chocolate milk and Ding Dongs (those delightful chocolate cakes filled with cream) to all the children, filling the journey with sweet anticipation.

Upon our arrival at the church, we were greeted by warm smiles and outstretched hands. One elderly gentleman, affectionately known as "Uncle Arthur," always had Juicy Fruit chewing gum for us kids. I would prance up and down the halls like an exuberant puppy, eagerly greeting everyone. Sunday was more than just a day of the week; it was a sanctuary of peace amid the chaos of my home. There was never a doubt that they loved me.

But some Sundays held an even more special place in my heart. Those were the Sundays when I had the privilege of spending the night at my grandaddy Frank's house. He was the pastor of a small country church in the quaint town of Peterson, Alabama.

---

1. Lesslie Newbigin, *Foolishness to the Greeks: The Gospel and Western Culture* (Grand Rapids: Wm. B. Eerdmans Publishing Co., 1986).

In the early days, that church lacked many modern amenities. It had wooden floors, no stained-glass windows, and not even indoor plumbing. I remember the chill that would greet us on cold winter mornings, with only a floor furnace to offer warmth. Even after it had warmed up, you could still feel the lingering cold drafts as the winter winds whispered through the cracks.

Hours later, the congregation would begin to arrive, and I would proudly introduce myself as Jeff, Grandaddy Frank's grandson. Grandaddy was known for his rhyming proclamations, and he would often say, "Jeff is growing tall as a wall," as I began to sprout upwards, or "That's Jeff right off the shelf." Shakespeare's legacy is definitely intact!

And then there was Sister Watts, with her blue hair neatly bundled in a bun. She always had her white handkerchief, which she would wave fervently during worship and at those powerful moments in my grandaddy's sermons when he'd become so impassioned about his Lord and Savior that he'd run back and forth across the tiny sanctuary, shouting, crying, laughing, and praising the Lord. He had a unique way of leading worship that I fondly refer to as "rare back." He would "rare back" and sing at the top of his lungs, "When we all get to heaven, what a day of rejoicing that will be. When we all see Jesus, we'll sing and shout the victory."

As time passed, Grandaddy took it upon himself to make improvements to the church. Bathrooms were added, a couple of Sunday school rooms, and even air-conditioning, all funded by his and my grandmother's modest earnings. I stood by his side as he hammered nails, cut two-by-fours, and even installed toilets. There were few men on this planet I would have rather spent time with.

Over forty years have passed since those days, but I can still almost smell the cold, musty, and dusty sanctuary of that old church when I close my eyes. I can vividly recall the cobwebs in the corners and see Grandaddy meticulously sweeping and mopping the church before services. Perhaps it was those experiences that ultimately shaped my passion and led me to heed God's call to plant churches.

As I penned this book about building tomorrow's church through love and presence, it was Frank who came to mind. Someone once asked me who had mentored me as I embarked on this project. Initially, I couldn't think of a specific person who had poured into my life. I was searching for a renowned professor, a distinguished pastor, or a high-profile leader like John Maxwell, someone with a glittering reputation and numerous books on the subject. But no one of that stature came to mind.

Yet, as I progressed in writing this book over the past year, it dawned on me that it was Frank—my grandfather—all along. Just as the Israelites missed recognizing Jesus as the Messiah because they had preconceived notions of the role of the Messiah, I had overlooked Grandaddy. Looking back, it seems so obvious, but my education had conditioned me to seek a specific model as a mentor, someone highly skilled. However, what I truly needed was love.

I miss those days dearly, and it's more than mere nostalgia. It's about how faith was passed down from one generation to the next. I observed as my grandfather spent hours at altars, kneeling beside his bed or turning his living room couch into a makeshift altar. Although he only had a third-grade education, he instinctively understood that what made a church holy was the presence of God. If God had promised to be with us wherever we went, then any place could become a holy place; we just needed to open our eyes.

I later learned that this concept was not new. In Gaelic folklore and Celtic mythology, there is a notion of "thin places" or "thin spots," "*àit-thighe*" (pronounced "atch-ee").[2] These are

2. Kenda Creasy Dean, *Almost Christian: What the Faith of Our Teenagers Is Telling the American Church* (New York, Oxford Press, 2010), 165

places where the boundary between the physical world (earth) and the spiritual world (heaven or the otherworld) is believed to be especially thin or permeable. In these places, it is thought that one can more easily connect with the divine, experience the supernatural, or have a heightened spiritual encounter.

Thin places, as I mentioned earlier, are often associated with natural features like ancient stones, sacred wells, caves, burial mounds, or specific landscapes with deep historical or mythological significance. It's fascinating to note that my grandaddy, despite knowing nothing about ancient Celtic mythology, instinctively recognized the presence of God in those moments. Oh, how I long for the days of that "old-time religion." Back then, theological debates on social media were unheard of; instead, we expressed our faith through the timeless hymns like "It Is Well with My Soul" and "Great Is Thy Faithfulness." Our Nazarene denomination's watchword and song, "Holiness unto the Lord," weren't just lyrics; they were a way of life.

Ultimately, the Holy Spirit worked through Frank's unwavering faithfulness, persistent presence, and tireless determination to transform the lives of others. It was Frank's love for my father, Doug, that led him from forbidding the mention of Jesus at our dinner table to echoing the words of Job within his Bible, declaring, "Though He slay me, I will serve Him." This transformation resulted in him surrendering his life to become a follower of Jesus and answering God's call to become a Nazarene pastor, in the very denomination whose churches he once vowed never to set foot in. Whoever claimed that God lacks a sense of humor or irony certainly didn't understand Him well.

Spiritual practices are profoundly important. Reading the Bible serves as a vital means of nurturing a significant Christian identity and preserving our legacies. Ultimately, the most impactful way to influence the next generation is to remain faithful and obedient to God's purpose and call in our own lives. We should invite them to walk the path of following Jesus alongside us. Seek to love them and meet them where they are, whether that's in a challenging neighborhood, a bar, or the local donut shop where you grab your morning coffee. I promise you that if you prioritize following Jesus, walking in the dust of the Rabbi, you won't need to worry about your legacy; it will naturally fall into place.

God didn't task us with growing the church; He commissioned us to make disciples. But unless we step out of silos of safety and venture into depths unknown, our footprints on the shores of eternity will be minimal. The next generation will continue to be shaped by forces outside the kingdom of God. So, where is God calling you? St. Irenaeus wisely stated, "The glory of God is man fully alive."[3] If you desire to bring glory to God, then live! Thrive! Reject mere survival and embrace a life of resurrection. Die to yourself daily and allow God to raise you from the dead. A Christian identity is best caught before it's taught, and a life lived passionately will be more impactful for the next generation than any virus or adversity.

The notion that professional clergy are the sole agents responsible for inviting and carrying out ministry is not a biblical idea; it's a construct of the church. The religious institutions of old set up barriers that prevented ordinary people from engaging in ministry. The ancient religious elite were the architects of exclusive systems that only permitted the best and the brightest to follow the Rabbi, sit at His feet, and learn. While their intentions may have been good—aiming to protect the faith—since when does God need humanity's protection? Wasn't it essential, in fact, a commandment, not to create graven images? Unlike other gods, Yahweh doesn't need to be pulled in a wagon into battle; He goes before us.

Jesus, in His ministry, called carpenters, fishermen, tax collectors, and even counted prostitutes among His most cherished followers. He achieved in three years what the priests and Pharisees hadn't accomplished in generations. They remained

3. St. Irenaeus, *Against Heresies*, Book 5, Chapter 6, Paragraph 1.

bound by the law, but Jesus set them free by fulfilling it. The term "laypeople" doesn't denote a separation between clergy and congregants; rather, it signifies the work of the people. In one of the churches where I served in my early ministry, located in an old mill town, laypeople were instrumental in its establishment. In fact, each little town had a textile mill, and each town had a church, many of which were planted by laypeople. The church in which I served was Shawmut. These textile mill workers initiated the church's founding, and the legend goes that they sent a letter to their district superintendent expressing the need for a church in Shawmut. The district superintendent's response? "Then start one!" And so, they did, erecting a tent, leading to a revival and the birth of a church.

I still witness such movements happening today, although not as prominently in the United States. I coach leaders worldwide on church planting. I work alongside them to clarify their vision and mission, crafting a four-phased plan from discerning God's call and context to launching the church. One leader I know wakes up every morning, takes a boat to small Indonesian islands, preaches the gospel, raises up leaders, and within weeks, a church is planted. Another is in Vietnam, having planted almost thirty churches in one year. African leaders, despite hostile environments, eagerly line up to be trained, and they, in turn, train others. They take the principle of multiplication seriously. Some are pastors, some are ordained, but most are ordinary individuals faithfully answering God's call on their lives.

So, I ask you, where is God calling you? Perhaps you're thinking, "Well, I'm a teacher, and God has called me to the classroom where we can't even pray." But you can! You may not be able to lead the prayer, but you can seize any opportunity, no matter how small, that a student opens. Students are naturally curious, and you can guide them through that door. Maybe you're an engineer, an entrepreneur, or someone with a ministry idea but unclear on its form. Let's talk! My contact information is in the back of this book, and you can find me online.

In closing, remember that "there are no superhero Christians who stand alone in faithfulness to God amidst persecution and suffering. Superhero Christians who rely solely on themselves don't exist, and they never have. It is by the power of the Holy Spirit that we are made faithful."[4] Allow me to share an anecdotal tale that, though its source is unknown, has been passed down:

The Man in the Mirror

A man lies on his deathbed, reflecting on his life and the dreams he had when he was young. He recalls that in his youth, he had grand ambitions to change the world, make a significant impact, and bring about positive transformation on a global scale. However, as he faces his final moments, he realizes that despite his lofty aspirations, he never accomplished the monumental changes he had envisioned.

With his last breaths, he comes to a profound realization: he could have made a difference in the world by changing himself. He recognizes that personal growth, self-improvement, and living in accordance with his values and principles could have had a ripple effect, inspiring and influencing others to do the same. In the end, he understands that changing the world begins with changing oneself.

If you aspire to make a meaningful impact on Christian identity, prioritize nurturing your relationship with the Lord and allow His love to overflow from your cup into the lives of others. Your personal transformation can ripple through the world around you. As you walk in the dust of the Rabbi, may you and those alongside you become covered in that holy dust together.

---

4. Dwight Gunter, *Seven Letters to Seven Churches* (Kansas City: Beacon Hill Press, 2011), 51

Table of Contents

Dedication - 5

Foreword - 7

Preface - 9

Acknowledgments - 11

Introduction - 13

Chapter 1. Reaching the Next Generations:
Building Relationships and Strong Bonds - 23

Chapter 2. Walking in Faith:
Welcoming The Next Generation into Covenant Relationship39

Chapter 3. Embarking into the Unknown:
Creating Sacred Spaces and Safe Places - 61

Chapter 4. Leading by Example:
Building Bridges to Culture and Community - 93

Chapter 5. Dancing with the Divine:
Embracing Christ's Example for Life Transformation - 111

Chapter 6. The Eternal Footprints of a Legacy:
Living the Journey of Faith - 129

Chapter 7. Unlocking Consequential Faith:
Discovering the Final Key - 163

Chapter 1

Reaching the Next Generations
Building Relationships and Strong Bonds

"The fruit of the righteous is a tree of life,
and the wise capture souls."[5]

Church Unchained—The Resurgence of Faith

That witty remark credited to Mark Twain, "The rumors of my demise are greatly exaggerated," might well be echoed by the church. If we're honest, there's a pervasive rumor mill whispering that the church is teetering on the brink of irrelevance. But this isn't a punchline; it's a heart-stopping, bone-chilling fear that races through our veins. We check the news like our lives depend on it, scanning the horizon of our churches, frantically wondering, "Where are the young folks?" or "Is the church really becoming a relic?" Will the church in America go the way of those in Europe and become museums or, worse, be retrofitted for some less purposeful use?

Of course, we turn to the gospel of research—Barna, Pew, Gallup—hoping against hope that these data deities might sing a different tune. Yet, they too seem to hum the dirge of the "nones," those religiously unaffiliated folks on the rise.[6] But wait, there's more! Dive a bit deeper into the rabbit hole of these stats, and you'll find a treasure trove of hope, the kind of hope that could make a superhero blush.

5. Proverbs 11:30 (NRSV)
6. Funk and Smith, in their work titled *"Nones" on the Rise"* published by Pew Research Center

Crafting Connections:
Building Bridges with the "Nones"

A closer look at the research data, and it's like those numbers are playing hide-and-seek with the real story. One Pew question asks people about their faith, and perhaps to one's surprise, a good number opt for the "no specific religion" label. Our first reaction is to panic. In a society bloated with information, along with those all too anxious to preside over the church's funeral, we might be tempted to take this at face value. As you look beneath the surface of the numbers, you realize it is not that they are devoid of faith. It's that they are deeply connected to each other; they are hedging their spiritual bets.[7] The plot twist is that they cherish their friendships more than Peter Parker loves his Spidey suit.

They are not willing to risk offending their friends by picking a faith card. They deeply value their connections to one another. They take friendships seriously. It's like asking a toddler to choose between his/her favorite toy and the beloved pet pug—not an easy choice. For them, Christianity is a lovingly demanding suitor, asking for exclusive devotion. But what the Christian faith often fails to do is help them recognize we are not asking them to abandon their friends. We're extending an invitation to follow Jesus to a life more abundant, a life bursting with meaning, a life free from the shackles of scarcity. If their friends don't want to come, that is okay. We can be confident that as they experience the transformative love of Jesus, He will transform their friends as well. Too often, we have treated our Christian faith like a cult. It is as if we're afraid these new babies in Jesus are going to catch cooties from the friends who don't share their faith. Here is where the narrative takes a thrilling turn—they're a generation that craves personal bonds like Indiana Jones yearns for adventure. You connect them with Jesus, and once they "taste and see the

---

7. Funk and Smith, in their work titled *"Nones" on the Rise"* published by Pew Research Center

Lord is good," they will be sharing this wholesome nourishment with all their friends. [8]

The Dance of Discipleship:
Tapping into a Deeper Connection

From a broader kingdom of God perspective, this has exciting implications. As much as the "nones" are a generation immersed in the virtual worlds of technology, they prefer face-to-face, heart-to-heart connections that break through the "no specific religion" wall.[9] When they don't have a personal connection to a faith, they would rather keep their spiritual options open.[10] We are not just talking about faith; we are talking about their very identity. And that is the church's golden ticket. They seem to instinctively recognize that the Christian faith at its core is rooted in Identity—at least it should be. They do not understand all the implications and connections to the entire kingdom of God, but unlike many in the older generations who have conflated Christianity with their country, they will not need to leap tall buildings in a single bound to make this connection. Instead, it's as if they have been given a roadmap through the maze with signposts clearly showing the way. They are uniquely shaped to be the source of the revival for which the church has been praying for as long as I have been living. Let us be sure we do not snuff out its flame because it doesn't look like previous revivals or meet our expectations.

The church stands to gain, and gain big, from these revelations. While the wider world scratches its head at the "nones," we can roll up our sleeves and give them something the world can't—personal connections and purpose. It's like handing a bottle

---

8. Psalm 34:8 (NRSV)
9. Funk and Smith, in their work titled *"Nones" on the Rise* published by Pew Research Center.
10. Ibid

of water to someone parched in the desert. They're parched for something deeper, and we've got the spiritual well.

The even better news? They're not just looking for connections; they're looking for real relationships. So, it's time for the church to transform into a sort of spiritual matchmaker, forging divine connections. But there's more to the story.

Prayer Power: The Ring of Power We've Had All Along

I'm an avid fantasy enthusiast, with *The Hobbit* and *The Lord of the Rings* trilogy ranking high among my favorites.[11] I have a penchant for finding intriguing parallels between these fantastical tales and the realm of the Christian faith. As some of you might already know, I spend a significant part of my time coaching pastors, particularly in the realm of church planting and revitalizing churches. So, when I'm not engrossed in my coaching duties, it's no surprise that my leisure hours often find me immersed in fantasy literature and movies.

In the world of *The Lord of the Rings*, there's a central focus on the One Ring that wields immense power.[12] Yet, there's more to the story. There was a total of twenty rings, including the infamous Ring of Power. Nine were bestowed upon men, seven upon dwarves, and three upon the elves. Sauron's Ring of Power, the twentieth, reigned supreme among them all.[13] However, what sets the elven rings apart is their unique nature. While they were still subject to the Ring of Power's influence, they lacked the malevolent magic of the others. Instead, their magic stemmed from Mithril—a force for good.[14]

---

11. J.R.R. Tolkien, *The Lord of the Rings*, 87. (New York: Houghton Mifflin, 1954)
12. J.R.R. Tolkien, *The Lord of the Rings*, 105. (New York: Houghton Mifflin, 1954)
13. J.R.R. Tolkien, *The Lord of the Rings*, 105. (New York: Houghton Mifflin, 1954)
14. J.R.R. Tolkien, *The Lord of the Rings*, 110. (New York: Houghton Mifflin, 1954)

These three elven rings, in particular, were crafted with the intent of preservation. They played a pivotal role in ensuring the elves' existence well into the third age, thanks to the Mithril they contained.[15] These rings gave life and maintained balance in the face of darkness. One ring had the power to corrupt, two could divide, but three together brought balance. They were a crucial defense against the corrupting influence of Sauron.[16]

In the church, we might draw a parallel to these elven rings when we consider our various programs. These programs serve to infuse purpose into people's lives, aid in the discipleship journey, and help individuals engage with the life of the church and the kingdom of God. In essence, they sustain the life of our congregation. However, it's essential to recognize that these programs, while valuable, are not the ultimate source of power.

Consequential Faith

While the reasons for the church's decline are complex, part of the blame lies in our tendency to reduce the Christian faith to what works instead of what is faithful. We cannot make a Faustian deal with the devil to grow our churches short term.[17] Just because something is expedient and appears to work on the surface does not mean it worked. The long-term consequences are a bastardization of the Christian faith. The church growth movement, which began in the 1960s, while well-meaning, often sought what worked over what was faithful to the kingdom of God. An at-all-costs approach to win the next generation is not an option. They will not respond to a meaningless faith. They are seeking a consequential faith that shapes their identity in

---

15. J.R.R. Tolkien, *The Lord of the Rings*, 117. (New York: Houghton Mifflin, 1954)

16. J.R.R. Tolkien, *The Lord of the Rings*, 118. (New York: Houghton Mifflin, 1954)

17. Johann Wolfgang von Goethe, *Faust* (New York: Penguin Classics, 2005).

transformative ways and has implications for the rest of their lives and their friends' lives.[18]

Perhaps we might say our equivalent of Mithril is the culture of prayer. I firmly believe that prayer is the vital link connecting us to the Spirit of God, offering us divine guidance. When prayer combines with our programs, it forms a formidable defense against the corrupting influences of the enemy, aiding us in discerning the will of God. Reaching those elusive next generations, especially the enigmatic Gen Z, starts with a simple prayer. A prayer for God to let us see through His eyes, a prayer to break our hearts for what breaks His. It may sound simple, but it's the first step in a grand adventure. *The Adventures of Indiana Jones* is a Saturday morning children's cartoon park compared to the adventure that awaits any of us who has the courage to pray such a prayer.

Making Room for the Next Generation(s)

Imagine the scene after Jesus' crucifixion, resurrection, and subsequent ascension to heaven. For His disciples and followers, it must have felt like a surreal and even cruel twist of fate. The emotional rollercoaster they endured, from the despair of Jesus' crucifixion to the astonishment of His resurrection, was enough to leave anyone bewildered. As they gathered in the aftermath, in the upper room, the atmosphere was undoubtedly charged with tension. Fresh memories of Jesus washing their feet mingled with the foreboding knowledge of His broken body and spilled blood during the Passover feast. It turned out that time in the upper room wasn't just any Passover; it was a profound foreshadowing of His crucifixion.[19]

Adding to the turmoil, the Roman Emperor had recently quashed a potential uprising, and his watchful eye now loomed over them. The upper room was a powder keg of emotions,

---

18. Funk and Smith, in their work titled *"Nones" on the Rise"* published by Pew Research Center
19. John 13:1–17 (NRSV)

potentially fraught with blame and recrimination. In the midst of this chaos, they prayed. And then, suddenly, a divine storm erupted. A howling wind and blinding light penetrated the room, cutting through the cacophony of their conversations. When the dust settled, tongues of fire rested upon each one of them, and they found themselves filled with the Holy Spirit, speaking in languages unknown to them. But the true miracle wasn't just the wind, fire, or newfound linguistic skills. The true miracle was the unity that emerged from this supernatural event. Despite their diverse backgrounds and languages, they understood each other perfectly. The Holy Spirit bridged the gaps that had once divided them.

In today's troubled world, what we need more than ever are personal "upper room" experiences. We need the Holy Spirit to infuse our conversations with hope and grace, creating an atmosphere where grace and mercy flow like boundless waters. It's in these sacred moments that God opens our ears and eyes to the needs of the next generations. If the Holy Spirit can bridge that cultural gap that existed in the upper room in the midst of such raw emotions, our faith should not waver that the Holy Spirit can bridge the current cultural gap that exists between the church and the next generation. So, pray earnestly for the Lord to weave your heart with theirs. Seek the Holy Spirit's guidance to instill your church with a profound sense of unity in your mission and vision for reaching these future generations.

I'm reminded of the story of Deana. Deana, a young Gen Z individual, had a challenging week. Interestingly, her journey to our church didn't involve a personal invitation or prior knowledge of how wonderful our congregation was. It was more akin to a random dart throw but in the modern age. Deana's tool of choice was Google Maps. She decided to explore the churches in her area, and as she examined the maps, something about our church's exterior caught her eye. Later, when Deana shared her experience, she recounted:

The people were very nice. Their arms were wide open and welcoming. This is nice. It feels like very homey, warm, and welcoming. I asked a lot of questions, and they were very patient with me and understanding. I hung around afterward, and when I walked outside after the eleven o'clock service, they were baptizing people. I asked what was going on, and someone told me they were baptizing people. They asked if I wanted to be baptized. I answered, "Well, yeah!"

"Okay, let's do it," the lady responded.

"Like right now? Today?"

Again, the lady responded, "Yeah!" I was baptized on the spot. The crowd went wild outside. Everyone knew who I was at this point. Everyone was cheering for me and were happy. It felt like a family. I feel like that was like a pivotal moment that just kept repeating, and repeating, and repeating. And then this happened, and that happened. I got involved in Bible studies. I received mentorship from Godly people who were walking in obedience with God. Kyra ended up mentoring me for that entire foundation study and even to this day, she was my first mentor in Christ. I have such a huge heart for her. I love you, Kyra! She's always so patient with my questions. I didn't even know Moses had a brother! For me, after I started to learn more about prayer and how powerful it really is. I would go into prayer like every single day and at the end of the day. I would kneel beside my bed and pray for the salvation of my family and loved ones. I know that is the most important thing because once that happens, God does the rest!

Nurturing Faith and Community: Deana's Impact on Generations

Deana's connection with Kyra was so profound that she often mentioned her by name, acknowledging Kyra as someone who had a significant impact on her spiritual journey. Remarkably, Deana's influence extended far beyond herself. Thanks to her, multiple family members have found salvation. Deana's aunt, a devoted Buddhist for over fifty-one years, initially resisted Deana's invitations to attend church. However, through Deana's persistence and the transformative power of her own faith, her aunt eventually joined her at church and became a follower of Jesus.

Deana, a young Gen Z member, has been an integral part of that church for over a year now. She reflects on her journey, saying, "It's incredible to look back and see how new I was to the faith." Deana grasps the significance of prayer and understands that much is in God's hands. Our role is simply to be obedient and pray. To me, her experience resonates as akin to an "upper room" encounter.

Have you noticed how many times Deana mentioned feeling at home? Have you heard her express how welcomed she felt? I admit I had reservations when they baptized her on the spot. But then the Holy Spirit reminded me that He is a far better teacher than I am, and I should trust Him to impart the true meaning of baptism to her. Deana's salvation did not occur at an outreach event. It wasn't the result of a program or a simple sinner's prayer. The key, it seems, lies in the church's culture of prayer. The leadership has instilled in their congregation the expectation that newcomers will arrive, and when they do, patience is the order of the day. We are to disciple them, introducing them to the authentic Jesus of the Bible—not the distorted version often portrayed in sensationalized media stories. We are to welcome them and create an environment where they feel like they've just arrived home. When they come, they will be hungry. Our task? Feed them!

In our technologically connected age, it's ironic that despite the ability to be virtually connected anytime and anywhere, we often find ourselves more divided and isolated than ever before. However, when we invite the Spirit of God into our lives, a transformative power of connection emerges. Being called to something greater than oneself is powerfully unifying. People will unite around a greater purpose. This power resides in personal relationships, and it all begins with prayer. Just as a plow tills the soil to prepare it for seeds, prayer not only softens our hearts but also paves the way for meaningful conversations. In the realm of Wesleyan theology, this is referred to as "prevenient grace," the grace that precedes our actions.[20]

Following prayer, the next step involves forging one-on-one relationships, the kind that runs deep. These relationships are like slow-cooked meals, not quick microwave fixes. It's essential to keep in mind that the next generation may approach these relationships with suspicion due to the negative perceptions surrounding the church. Once trust has been established, the process of discipleship begins. (I will delve into the importance of a robust discipleship curriculum in a later chapter.) Taking a page from Jesus' playbook, who had twelve disciples as part of His team but poured into three deeply, we recognize that the next generation yearns for meaning. Currently, this quest for meaning often translates into seeking likes and follows on social media platforms. Unfortunately, the enemy has misled them into believing that becoming influencers or achieving TikTok fame will fulfill their lives. In reality, this pursuit often amounts to empty calories—spiritual junk food. Discipling the next generation involves providing them with the sustenance they crave. Just as a baby needs to learn how to eat, we must feed them spiritually first so they can understand what and how to feed their souls. We should not merely entertain them, as psychologists caution against placing iPads or iPhones in the hands of infants for pure amusement. In the same way, we should avoid parking them in front of the television all day to watch seemingly educational but ultimately shallow content. Babies thrive on personal interaction

20. John Wesley, "On Working Out Our Own Salvation," in *The Works of John Wesley*, Ser. 2, Vol. 2, ed. Albert C. Outler (The Journal of the WESLEYAN THEOLOGICAL SOCIETY, Volume 36, Number 1, Spring 2001), 29-39, Wesleyan Theological Society, P. O. Box 144, Wilmore, Kentucky 40390.

with their parents, and so does the next generation. Through two years of research, experiences, methods, and relationships, it became evident that meaningful connections with Christians who genuinely walk with Jesus play a pivotal role in shaping the spiritual identity of the next generations.

Have we, perhaps, misunderstood those Christians who attend our churches for a while and then depart? Could it be that they are yearning for authentic relationships? It's imperative to assess the "how" we are discipling people. The church is great at creating formulas and has done a magnificent job of institutionalizing Christianity. Unfortunately for us, the Bible does not say that God sent His only son so that whosoever believes in Him may one day become part of a venerable institution. Are we merely offering an array of programs and tools to distract them with entertainment, avoiding the complexities of one-on-one relationships?

Regardless of how proficient we become at entertaining people, our churches will never surpass the allure of worldly entertainment. This could be a significant factor in their departure. We may provide a buffet of entertainment, but it will never be as satisfying as a home-cooked meal, rich with nourishment and seasoned with tender, loving care.

Think about Thanksgiving at Grandma's house—everyone indulges in a hearty meal and then takes a well-deserved nap; we receive the proper nourishment and experience, that comforting sense of belonging and safety. What if our churches were determined to be spiritual grandparents' homes? We might even discover existing Christians, hungry for such a relationship, who haven't yet found a church that offers it. Could it be they still haven't found what they are looking for? I can assure you that once they find personal connection within the church, they will start identifying with the church family, growing, and nourishing others. We may find that our churches cannot contain the multitude of disciples we are making, necessitating the planting of new churches every six months to accommodate them.

For Deana, her journey began with transformation, and she was equipped with the tools. She was mentored through a personal relationship, thanks to her spiritual connection with Kyra. The next generation has access to a wealth of knowledge and programs, but what they truly hunger for is wisdom. Let us pray for the Holy Spirit's guidance and transformation in ourselves, enabling us to connect genuinely with others in the church. Let us seek divine direction on how to personally engage and communicate with the next generation, both within the church and in our families. We should implore God to lead us to someone for whom we can become a spiritual grandparent, nurturing their spiritual growth and well-being.

The Table of the Lord

There's a powerful song composed by the worship band at 12 Stone Church in Atlanta, Georgia. I find that its lyrics beautifully encapsulate the notion of nurturing the next generation while also serving as a poignant reminder that we should not anticipate from God anything for the upcoming generations that He hasn't already imparted upon us. As the father of two adopted children who emerged from exceedingly neglectful and abusive backgrounds, the concept of being embraced by God resonates deeply with me. Standards for loving and loving have radically decreased over the last two decades. I'm not alluding to shifts in financial standards of living, but rather, relationally. This song delves into the profound idea of God's grace reaching out to us and them long before we even consciously recognize it, embracing us as one of His own. I was unable to obtain permission for all of the lyrics, but here are a couple of relevant lines. I encourage you to look the rest up online. Search 12Stone worship on YouTube and Table of the Lord. Plus these two lines from song for which I was able to obtain permission:

And oh, grace undeserving, and freedom unending, I am your child forever. You love me as you found me, where I am invited, here to your table.

Surely, if the Lord invited us to His table, He asks us to invite the next generations and make room for them at His table as well? They are no less deserving than we are. God is inviting them to the table of the Lord, and he asks us to hand-deliver that invitation.

End of Chapter 1 Summary: Reaching the Next Generation

Despite prevailing assumptions and a substantial body of research, it is evident that the younger generations hold a keen interest in matters of faith and possess a spiritual identity, albeit not exclusively Christian. While they harbor significant reservations about institutionalized religion, these doubts are not confined to the Christian faith alone. Their hunger extends to the realms of faith, purpose, and establishing meaningful connections with older generations. In a world teeming with information, what they truly seek is wisdom. Remarkably, prayer emerges as the linchpin, the singular force that should underpin all endeavors of Christian leadership. While it might appear commonplace and self-evident, the emphasis placed on prayer in Jesus' ministry and its pivotal role in the birth of the church at Pentecost reinforces its enduring importance for the contemporary church.

Principles for Budling Strong Bonds with the Next Generations

Principle 1: Sacrifice Your Time and Comfort
Living out our faith and following God's will can be inconvenient and challenging. When guiding others in their faith journey:
- Be willing to learn alongside them. Embrace their questions, and if you don't have the answers, seek guidance from the Bible.

- Don't hesitate to involve other Christian leaders or pastors when needed. No one expects you to have all the answers.
- Prioritize honesty and authenticity to earn their trust and loyalty. Their trust can lead to them becoming powerful advocates for Christ.

Principle 2: Develop a Missionary Mindset

Instead of a self-serving approach, embrace a missionary mindset to share the message of Christ:
- Avoid divisive political discussions as they can deter people from focusing on Jesus.
- Share your personal Christian experiences, celebrate your church, and highlight the transformative power of God in your life on social media.

Principle 3: Shaping Identity in Christ

Once you've built relationships and overcome fears, the process of shaping your Christian identity becomes straightforward:
- Embody the qualities of God's people.
- Pray for guidance and opportunities from God.
- Share your own faith journey and encourage them to follow Jesus.
- Embrace the call to make disciples of everyone, reflecting God's image in your actions.

By following these principles, you can effectively impact the lives of those you are reaching out to and help shape their identities in Christ-like ways. These principles can help you effectively impact lives and shape Christian identities in others.

A Prayer for Reaching the Next Generations

Lord, give us Your eyes.

Break our hearts for the things that break Yours. Give us a burden so heavy for the future generations, the spiritually curious. May our churches be awakened to the hunger of those around us. Lord, help us to die to ourselves and surrender our will to Yours. Forgive us for our near-sightedness and for the comfort of our echo chambers. Lord, help us to remember that it is not the amount of debt we are forgiven but that we all had debt that we could not repay, but for Your grace and mercy.

Amen.

Reachable Questions for Reflection

1. Can you think of someone whom you had a meaningful relationship with that was key to your own spiritual journey?
2. Can you think of three people from the next generation that God might be asking you to mentor? If not, pray and ask God to send you opportunities.
3. Without being negative, what are some things your church can change that might be seen as an obstacle to reaching the next generations and moving forward?
4. Do you like the idea of a church full of spiritual grandparents? What do you think would happen in your church if you got the reputation in your community of being full of spiritual grandparents?

Chapter 2
Walking in Faith
Welcoming The Next Generation
into Covenant Relationship

"The outsider dwelling among you shall be to you as the native-born among you. You should love him as yourself—for you dwelled as outsiders in the land of Egypt. I am Adonai *your God"* [21]

Introduction

A quote often attributed to Mother Theresa says, "If we lack peace, it is because we have forgotten that we belong to each other." As I've mentioned before, connecting with the next generations, especially Gen Z, hinges on a fundamental need: the desire to belong. What sets them apart is that they're the first generation to grow up in a fully digital world. Imagine this: by the time they were eight or nine years old, they had already been exposed to things that previous generations didn't encounter until they were fourteen or fifteen. They've had more information at their fingertips than I had access to in an entire encyclopedic library, and theirs wasn't just text—it was video, interactive, and instantly accessible.

However, this remarkable access to knowledge came at a cost, and that cost was their childhood. They lost their innocence at a younger age, and the events of the last two years have only made it worse. With the ongoing impact of COVID-19, even as the world resumes some sense of normalcy, the effects linger. In many

---

21. Leviticus 19:34 (TLV)

places, the trauma associated with COVID-19 was compounded by sensationalized media coverage that thrived on fear for the sake of ratings. The result? Gen Z is now the most anxious generation, and this anxiety contributes to a profound sense of isolation.

Reflecting on the story of Deana from the first chapter, we can't help but remember her boundless excitement when she was baptized on her very first Sunday with us. Remember I confessed to being a bit judgmental in the moment. I questioned whether the church should baptize her without a full theological understanding of the act. However, the Holy Spirit swiftly checked my judgment. Deana may not have grasped the profound theological significance of her baptism right then, but she wholeheartedly comprehended its social significance. Baptism signified something crucial to her—it meant that she belonged!

This recollection brings me to a critical point: if we desire the next generations to feel genuinely welcome in our churches, we must actively cultivate a culture of belonging. When we make the younger generations feel like they belong, our doors will not be able to keep them out, and they'll bring many of their friends along.

Despite all the pessimistic headlines about the next generations, I hold a strong belief that God will work through Gen Z to bring about transformative changes in the church. I believe the church stands on the brink of another great awakening, and perhaps, even a day akin to Pentecost—a day where the Holy Spirit's presence becomes so undeniable that "at the name of Jesus every knee should bend, in heaven and on earth and under the earth, and every tongue should confess that Jesus Christ is Lord, to the glory of God the Father."[22] The recent "outpouring," as many called it, on the campus of Asbury University is at least anecdotal evidence of this belief.

It is of utmost importance that we interpret the above verse within its proper context. Far too often, the church has led with judgment before love, or at least judgment as it is often misun-

22. Philippians 2:9–11 (NRSV)

derstood. We have a tendency to conflate God's judgment with His wrath, assuming they are one and the same. However, they are fundamentally different. God's judgment is inherently salvific; it represents His initial act of salvation, always driven by the intent to rescue. God's actions are rooted in His boundless mercy. While it is possible to cherry-pick scriptures out of context that depicts an angry God punishing disobedience, a comprehensive reading of the Bible reveals a consistent pattern: when there is a contest between God's wrath and His love, His love and mercy invariably prevail.

This is not to suggest that we are immune to the consequences of our choices when we reject His love and mercy. When we do so, we bear the natural consequences of our actions, much like a child who, despite being warned not to touch a hot stove, is inevitably burned by their disobedience. In this analogy, the stove, not the parent, inflicts the injury. Moreover, the parent does not take delight in the child's suffering; they experience genuine compassion and empathetic pain, suffering alongside their child. Similarly, God reacts to our disobedience with sorrow, not with punitive wrath. I digress from further delving into biblical exegesis, as this is not a dissertation on the subject. Nevertheless, for those curious and motivated to explore it further, biblical hermeneutics can be profoundly enriching. I embarked on this brief diversion only to illustrate how erroneous theology can adversely impact our relationships.

The prostration of individuals before God is not merely fear but rather a profound sense of gratitude and awe, a response to His holiness. God's judgment is not akin to "Sauron's eye," menacingly surveilling us from above to be feared.[23] Rather, it is an act of love, earnestly urging us to return home. God is akin to the father in the parable of the prodigal son, watching from the doorway. Upon spotting his wayward child, the father rushes to embrace him, rejoicing in his return.

---

23. J.R.R. Tolkien , *The Lord of the Rings*.

Make Them Feel Like They Belong

Should you ever find yourself with the opportunity to visit some of the grand cathedrals scattered throughout Europe, I wholeheartedly encourage you to seize that chance. These architectural marvels stand as some of humanity's most awe-inspiring creations. Their spires ascend towards the heavens, their arches invoke imagery of celestial gates, and their colossal stained-glass windows narrate tales of hope to those within their sacred walls. These windows serve as enduring reminders of the biblical narrative, particularly the life of Jesus, and offer profound meaning to us. They not only recall the scriptural story but also emphasize that we are integral parts of His narrative, adopted into the family of God without preconditions.

Yet, in many ways, this narrative is akin to a family conversation. We (the church) possess our own unique culture, cherishing the sharing of our stories amongst ourselves. To outsiders, those unfamiliar with our tales, it can appear as though we inhabit a closed culture. For these individuals, the unfamiliarity with our stories can lead to feelings of isolation, confusion, and even rejection. To bridge this gap, we must invest time in teaching those on the outside about our stories and intentionally include them in our community. Otherwise, the cherished stained glass, which captivates us with its kaleidoscope of colors, may, to those on the outside, appear as a jumbled, chaotic mishmash of hues.

Without a biblical worldview, the images lose meaning and function as icons—pointers to something greater. These icons are like our family stories, meaningful because of the love within them.

God's Invitation: Unconditional Love

God invited us into His family without prerequisites, demonstrating His unconditional love. He didn't require us to understand all the family stories or adopt His culture beforehand. Instead, He showed us patience and sent us teachers, gave us His Word, and encouraged us to share His light. As members of God's family, we shouldn't act as gatekeepers, deciding who's in or out and setting the rules. God's invitation is extended to all. The decline in church attendance among the next generations isn't due to a lack of faith but is at least partially attributed to a sense of feeling unwelcomed and judged. Once more, I am not suggesting that anything goes. I am suggesting that we should not insist that they have Jesus figured out before we welcome them. We also must forget the notion that life must center around the church. The Christian life is centered around Jesus. The church is one means of grace that facilitates that relationship, but it is not the only means of God's grace.

On the Outside Looking In

Dear Evan Hansen is a musical and later a film that tells the story of Evan Hansen, a high school student dealing with social anxiety and loneliness. The story takes a dramatic turn when a letter he wrote to himself as part of his therapy is mistaken for a suicide note belonging to Connor Murphy, one of his classmates who took his own life. Evan gets caught in a web of lies and deception as he becomes involved with the Murphy family and pretends to have been Connor's close friend. The musical explores themes of mental health, isolation, the impact of social media, and the complexities of human relationships. It delves into Evan's journey to find his own identity and the healing power of honesty and connection.[24]

Evan Hansen is an uneasy outsider who longs for connection in the face of the social media age's instability and cruelty. A letter he wrote for an assignment ends up in the hands of a distraught couple whose son committed suicide, and from there, he sets out on a voyage of self-discovery. One of the more popular songs from the soundtrack is "Waving Through a Window." The song is a popular song among the next generations. In the song Evan

---

24. *Dear Evan Hansen*, directed by Michael Greif (2021; Film).

Hansen laments how he has learned to not even try to fit in, as he always ends up on the outside looking in. The chorus goes:

On the outside, always looking in; will I ever be more than I've always been? Cause I'm tap, tap, tapping on the glass. I'm waving through a window. I try to speak, but nobody can hear, so I wait around for an answer to appear while I'm watch, watch, watching people pass, I'm waving through a window. Oh, can anybody see, is anybody waving back at me? We start with stars in our eyes. We start believing that we belong. But every sun doesn't rise, and no one tells you where you went wrong.[25]

Are we hearing their cries for attention? While the song is not intended to describe the relationship between Christian identity and the next generations, I believe it is a window into their souls. After all, it is written by them, for them, and about them. It is their entertainment. Pay attention to the entertainment that people ingest; they are telling you something about themselves. Gen Z is determined to make their mark on the world. They are lonely and hungry for a life of significance and meaning. Many feel as if the church has left them on the outside looking in, and I am afraid we have been too busy admiring the rich echoes of our own voices while singing our own songs to notice them. The church needs to be all about hello. We must create a culture of what I am calling covenant hospitality.

A Culture Built on Covenant Principles
Covenant Hospitality

"Culture eats strategy for breakfast" is a phrase widely attributed to Peter Drucker. Although he did not actually ever say those words, the sentiment is true, regardless of whether it is a church, small group, small business, or Fortune 500 corporation. Even if they have a one-, five-, and ten-year plan, with input

---

25. Pasek, Benj, and Paul Justin. "Waving Through A Window." Performed by Ben Platt. 2017. Audio recording.

from some of their best strategic thinkers, if they fail to change the culture, their plans will fail. They can be well financed, well managed, with high-capacity leadership, but a toxic culture or even a culture out of sync with the strategy will fail. We often think that strategy shapes culture or a great marketing plan will drive results, but the truth is culture is the key component for leading change within an organization. A failure to change the culture will always result in a failure to change the organization.

Often, within a declining church, the problem is not so much a bad culture, though in some cases this might be true, but a comfortable culture. Church is and should be like a family. We want it to be a place where everyone is loved and can be themselves. A healthy family loves unconditionally. They accept us along with our flaws but are always encouraging us to grow and be a better version of ourselves. There are certain characteristics of the family that must be present for those conditions to exist. Comfort is one, but more than comfort, it is trust.

Expect tension. When strangers (outsiders) are welcomed into the family, they upset our equilibrium. Strangers can be perceived as a threat to existing relationships, and within the church, a threat to our existing power or position. It makes it difficult to trust, but that is exactly what we, as the people of God, are called to do. Moreover, it is essential that we engage in the discipleship of the next generation, ensuring they understand God's trustworthiness. We should not take for granted that they possess a biblical worldview or even basic biblical knowledge. This effort is aimed at creating space within our faith community and hearts for the upcoming generations.

Culture isn't just a bystander; it's the stage director of our success story and the lens through which we view the world. These lenses, tinted by our cultural backgrounds, paint our perception of reality. When it comes to contemporary Christianity, there's a yawning chasm between us and the ancient cultures that birthed the Bible. This gap doesn't diminish the Bible's relevance; it simply issues a clarion call for intentional interpretation and profound understanding.

Imagine hospitality in biblical times as a performance, always taking cues from the Exodus saga and later, the drama of exile. To grasp the true essence of these biblical narratives, we must put on our cultural archaeologist hats and embark on a quest to unearth the rich layers of historical context.

Obviously, trust must be a key component of hospitality. If one cannot trust that he/she will be safe, one will not feel welcome. We can trust God because God has proven to be trustworthy time and time again. God welcomed us into His family despite our being unworthy. God made covenant with Abraham, knowing Abraham could not possibly live up to his responsibility and the implications of the covenant. There is a lot of theology to unpack with the covenant between Abraham and God. This book is not a theological treatise on the covenant, but it is important for context. To understand the lengths God went to prove to Abram that He was trustworthy, we must have a firm understanding of the gravity and significance of the Abrahamic covenant.[26]

Certainly, trust stands as the bedrock of hospitality. In its absence, the welcome mat turns to quicksand, and a sense of safety becomes an elusive specter. In God, we find a paragon of trustworthiness, a luminary of fidelity whose track record speaks volumes. God flung open the doors of His family, bidding us welcome despite our unworthiness.

Consider the covenant cut between God and Abraham, a covenant of profound importance and far-reaching implications. While the theological depths of this covenant could fill volumes, our focus here is not a theological treatise. However, it's imperative to acknowledge its context. To fully grasp the lengths to which God went to demonstrate His trustworthiness to Abraham, we must appreciate the gravity and significance of the Abrahamic covenant.

---

26. Genesis 15:18–21 (NRSV)

Trust, the bedrock of vulnerability, invites us to bare our souls to one another, to embrace candor, and to extend our care and protection. In the nurturing embrace of a healthy family, we find solace in the knowledge that we have allies, guardians who stand by our side if our actions remain within the bounds of morality and legality. Moreover, we anticipate our family to act as our constructive critics, pushing us to grow and improve.

Yet, let us not forget that trust, like a delicate thread, weaves in both directions. For Gen Z, trust is an invaluable gift. Once squandered, it's seldom rekindled, and loyalty often goes with it. Therefore, we must hold their trust as a precious divine endowment, for indeed, it is.

The covenant between God and Abram transcended its immediate participants. While covenants were a customary practice between kings and kingdoms, they typically did not extend to weaker parties, especially not when the kings had little to gain. These covenants were often described as "cutting a covenant," resembling modern legal contracts, but exacted a cost far surpassing mere monetary or legal disputes. They were contracts sealed in blood.

God's covenant with Abram went beyond a mere land gift; it symbolized Abram's possession of a land he had not toiled for, complete with cities he had not constructed, and the privilege to dwell and partake in the fruits of vineyards and olive groves he had not planted. In this context, hospitality meant God welcomed Abram into a relationship mirroring the unity within the Trinity. Despite having nothing of worldly value to offer or even relationally, Abram received this remarkable inheritance as part of his inclusion in God's family, a divine blessing encompassing land and children.

This promise was nothing short of astronomical. It was customary with these types of covenants for each party to offer a tangible sign of commitments. Thus, God cut a covenant with

Abram.[27] This is the divine hospitality God modeled for us. We should expect to offer nothing less to the next generations as we seek to cut our covenant with them.

Ten Aspects of Covenant from Which We Can Learn

1. A New Identity Is Made

There were ten parts to an ancient covenant. The first action that would take place between the covenant partners is that they would swap garments. This was an attempt to confuse the identities. It was symbolic for swapping identities. A symbol that they are becoming one. When it comes to Gen Z, identity is a complicated subject and area that will challenge the church's biblical worldview. According to a recent Gallup survey, one in five adults from Gen Z identify as LGBTQ, with bisexual being the most common.[28]

Most Christians would agree that the LGBTQ lifestyle is contrary to the will of God and, therefore, is sin. They would agree with the statement that the LGBTQ lifestyle runs counter to a biblical worldview. As Christians, we must tread carefully on this issue with the next generations. One of the fears or complaints that I hear often from inside the local church is that the institutional church is making compromises in faith in an attempt to remain relevant. Christians do not have to compromise their beliefs to reach the next generations. We *can* compromise our reactions. When ministering to someone who is LGBTQ, I keep these things in mind:

1. As Christians, remember our first call is to love our neighbor as ourselves. There are a lot of things my neighbor may do that I may not agree with.
2. Sin is sin, regardless of the type of sin. The Western church tends to elevate sexual sins above other sins. Let us remember all sin is equal in the eyes of God, though

---

27. Genesis 15:18–21 (NRSV)
28. Jones, "LGBT Identification in U.S. Ticks Up to 7.1%." Gallup News.

it may have different consequences. We sometimes forget sin is its own punishment. Let us grieve all sin, including our own, but continue to love like Jesus.

3. Remember, they do not necessarily arrive with a biblical worldview. We cannot expect the next generations to share our biblical worldview if they are spiritually unresolved as it relates to a relationship with Jesus.

4. Preach, teach, and model holiness. I want to emphasize *model*. Remember Jesus' warning to remove the plank from one's own eye before judging someone else.[29] We look rather foolish teaching people to remove specks from their eyes, regardless of the nature of the speck, when we are walking around with canoes on our own.

Because the next generations value others so highly, as well as the fact they are so collaborative, this is a key component of earning their trust and helping them feel welcome.

They will not risk associating their identity with Christians if they do not feel valued and trusted. Wagging our fingers in their faces, insisting they conform to our way of thinking the moment they enter the walls of our church will almost guarantee they never return. They will simply be another story, another body on the cultural landscape of the narratives that the church cannot be trusted. Another victim who was hurt by the church while simultaneously confirming the caricatures of the church they had already seen. Be as patient with them as God was with Abram.

When God cut the covenant with Abram, Abram was placed into a deep sleep. God was the only one who walked between the cut heifer because only God would be able to be faithful to the covenant. Had Abram also walked in between the two halves, once he broke the covenant, death would have been his punishment. Perhaps we might think, well, God could just forgive, but that was not the nature of the old covenant. There was not provision for

---

29. Matthew 7:5 (NRSV)

the forgiveness of the other party, otherwise the covenant would have been meaningless. Had Abram broken the covenant and if God did not keep His word and kill Abram, God would have been demonstrating He was not trustworthy. We should keep this at the top of our minds when ministering to any generation.

2. Power is Shared

The second part of the covenant would be the swapping of each party's belts. This was a symbol of exchanging strengths, assets, and resources. It was a symbol of shared power and influence. This is not just swapping but the equivalent of joining strength, assets, and resources. If the church wants the next generations to feel welcome, it will not only welcome the next generation's attendance, but it will also invite their involvement. They will listen to their suggestions. While we think of generosity in terms of wealth, giving away one's power is the ultimately act of generosity. It is also an act of trust. We also must be generous with our time. Do not just invite them to be part of your church; invite them to be part of your life. They are not interested in a once-a-week relationship. If we want to influence the next generations, we must spend time with them. Let down your emotional walls and allow them in. Open our lives to them and open our minds to them. Be generous with our mercy. Take the posture of a servant, not a college professor. They have Google if they want more information. They need us to model holiness. Google definitely cannot provide that.

The institutional church, as well as the local church, must embrace this same culture of hospitality modeled by God and then in the person of Jesus. If we are to be the body of Christ, it begins with a culture of covenant hospitality.

3. Protection and Loyalty Are Given

The third step of the Covenant was an exchange of weapons. This was symbolic of the exchange of enemies. Perhaps we might see this as an ancient form of a military alliance. It was a commitment to loyalty—a public testimony that each party to the covenant had the other's back. I said it already, but the next generations are fiercely loyal. Demonstrate to them that you genuinely see them as people, not a target. Communicate empathy and compassion for their circumstances. Remember, they are anxious. The church is called "sanctuary" because we are supposed to be a shelter for the lost and lonely. We are sanctuary because we offer protection for the huddled masses yearning to live free.

4. Unconditional Love Is Present

The fourth step of cutting the covenant was the cutting of the heifer into two halves. In a blood covenant, something had to die. Each half of the cow would be placed on each side, and both parties would walk between the halves, blood side up. This was a public statement that if either party were to violate the covenant, that person was committing to the same fate as the cow. On its face, this does not sound like love, but remember, before the ceremony began, God caused Abram to fall into a deep sleep.

The next generations, Millennials and Gen Z, are by and large unfamiliar with unconditional love. A recent survey commissioned by British media outlet Channel 4 reported Gen Z (a quarter) were less tolerant and supportive of limits on free speech.[30] Almost half agreed some people were more likely to believe people should be canceled.[31] They have been able to customize their lives to their liking. They can customize music, clothing, and through social media friends. Exposure to different perspectives builds tolerance since they have not been exposed to ideas and preferences outside of themselves; it explains why they are less tolerant.

My suggestion is not that we treat them like petulant children and cater to their every whim. Healthy boundaries need to be taught and we need to embrace them. Neither am I suggesting the church should compromise our ethics and core values as long

---

30. Revoir, "Gen Z Are 'less Tolerant' of Other People's Views than Their Elders." The Daily Mail.
31. Ibid.

as they are consistent with Jesus' command, "Love God with all our heart mind, and strength and love your neighbor as yourself." I am suggesting we model God's covenant with Abram. We offer unconditional love regardless of how many times they break covenant with us. As we embody covenant hospitality in our churches, they will take notice of our holiness. They will recognize we are unique and set apart. When we embody covenant hospitality, they hear our invitation to be holy as God is holy.

5. A Mark Is Made

The fifth step would be a covenant mark would be made. In ancient times the hand was considered all the way down past the wrist. Each party would slice their wrist, commingle their blood, then rub dirt into the wound. This had the effect of creating a mark/scar. It is as if they would be carrying their contract with them everywhere they go. It also was a warning to others not to mistreat a man of a covenant. He is not to be trifled with because someone has his back.

God marked Abram with circumcision. A male child was considered the greatest gift a god could give a man. Children were their progeny. Male children carried their name into the future, thus giving them abundant life. God marked Abram in the place where he would have the constant reminder that God gave him the gift of abundant life. He gave him a male child. Even after the child was gone, Abram would always be reminded of his covenant with God.

What is the mark Christians will make in covenant with the next generation? They are determined to leave their mark on society.

6. One Must Lay Down One's Life: "I present my body a living sacrifice" (Romans 12:1).

The sixth step of cutting the covenant was the walk of death. Both parties travel in the figure eight, the infinity symbol, and walk in between the two halves of the calf. The symbolism here was if either of them broke the covenant in any way, then he would suffer the same fate as the heifer.

Abram was unable to walk because God had placed him in a deep sleep. God knew Abram would never be able to remain faithful to the covenant. Had Abram walked between the two halves the first time he was unfaithful according to the rules of the covenant relationship, Abram would have had to have been killed. Only God walked between the two halves; thus, God accepted both sides of the covenant. Therefore, when Abram or his children broke the covenant, God had to make the sacrifice. God entered into a covenant with Abram for the purpose of rescuing the world, knowing it would eventually cost Him His life. Let us not let His sacrifice be in vain.

In another famous prayer of Jesus, on the eve of His capture and subsequent crucifixion, He prayed to the Father on behalf of the disciples. In the moments leading up to this, He tells them, "This is my commandment, that you love one another as I have loved you. No one has greater love than this, to lay down one's life for one's friends."[32] We must lay down our lives for the next generations. I cannot tell you exactly how that looks in your context. But I can imagine it will not take long to understand what God is calling you to do.

7. Blessing Is Given

The seventh step was to pronounce blessings and curses. Part of the walk of death was to pronounce blessings and curses upon each other as you walked between the heifer. As they walked, they would say may you be blessed as long as you remain faithful to this covenant, but may you and all you love be cursed and like the animal on the ground if you do not.

As we enter into relationship with the next generations, we need to practice seeing what is right in their lives and keep our focus there. Christians, especially in the older generations, will

---

32. John 15:12–13 (NRSV).

not have to look hard to find something that they believe with which we disagree. Learn the art of prayer's lament. They will be helpful as we grieve the loss of the old, but God will simultaneously give us the grace to adapt to the new. Be intentional about praying and pronouncing blessings over the next generations. I do not mean empty accolades. I mean, pray for God to help you see them through the eyes of Jesus. You will not be disappointed.

8. Serving Others First

The eighth step was a covenant meal. At the covenant meal, each party to the covenant would feed the other one the first bite. This was a further symbol of unity and care. It was to say, I am putting your needs before my own.

"Jesus, knowing that the Father had given all things into his hands and that he had come from God and was going to God, got up from supper, took off his outer robe, and tied a towel around himself. Then he poured water into a basin and began to wash the disciples' feet and to wipe them with the towel that was tied around him."[33]

A Basin, a Water Pitcher, and a Towel

I heard a pastor preach a unique Easter sermon once. It centered around being servants in the kingdom of God. The opening of the sermon went something like this.

There sat at the entrance to the door—a basin, a water pitcher, and a towel—all used for the washing of the feet of the guests as they entered a home after travel on the dank, dusty, and dangerous Palestinian roads—a basin, a water pitcher, and a towel. It was the sign of generous hospitality. It was what servants did; only servants used the basin, the water pitcher, and the towel as they washed and dried their feet. Washing feet was reserved for those of the lowest status and position in the culture; it was reserved for those who had no claim to dignity, worth, value, or honor that anybody was bound to

---

33. John 13:3–5 (NRSV).

respect. Only those of little value and worth used the basin, the water pitcher, and the towel. There sat at the entrance to the door—a basin, a water pitcher, and a towel as the disciples came into the home. They did not see anyone to handle the basin, the water pitcher, and the towel.

It was not their task, thought the disciples. It was not their duty. It was not their responsibility. In some ways, it was beneath them. They were not servants. They were more interested in being served, and so as they entered the home, the basin, the water pitcher, and the towel sat there.[34]

Jesus and the Father had been present at the Abrahamic covenant. They knew this day would come. It was time for God to reap what Abram and the rest of humanity had sown. They had broken covenant, and God had to pay up. Jesus saw the reluctance of the disciples to serve but knew His time with them was coming to a close. He had yet another lesson to model for them. His introspective question of the disciples is also a call for us in the church to do some introspection as well. What pitchers, towels, and basins are sitting at the door of our churches unused because it is not our job?

His leaving and His purpose were on His mind. He looked and saw the basin, the water pitcher, and the towel. He got up from the meal, took off His outer clothing, and wrapped a towel around His waist. After that, He poured water into a basin and began to wash His disciples' feet. Is this how kings act? Is this how the King of Kings and the Lord of Lords acts? It is not how earthly kings act, but it is how the King of Kings who made a covenant with Abram and His descendants acts, and how He calls His church to act. Wash the feet of the next generations. Show them how the people of God plan to rule. Show them we are holy. Show them we are set apart for a purpose, and so are they.

---

34. Frank Thomas Preaching Coach "A Basin, Water Pitcher, and a Towel", 14:57 https://www.youtube.com/watch?v=hkZXiB7S0VA

9. A Family is Formed

The ninth part of the covenant was the exchange of names. Each would leave carrying a part of each other's name. Each time, someone would say the other's name. In Genesis 17, God changes Abram's name to Abraham. Every time someone spoke Abraham's name post-covenant, they were speaking God's name. When Moses encountered God in Exodus 3 at the burning bush, God said, "I am the God of Abraham."[35] In other words, I am the God who made covenant with Abraham.

I have already said it multiple times, but the defining trait of Gen Z is they want to belong. If we create a culture of covenant hospitality, they will gladly take on the name of Christ and join the family.

10. Self-Sacrifice As Seed for the Next Generations

The final element of the covenant involves the exchange of the oldest male son. This act symbolizes the giving of one's future, essentially saying, "I am giving you my life, and our families are forever entwined." This aspect of covenant hospitality is the most profound, signifying that our lives are no longer our own but bound to others. It's the heart of the covenant.

In this context, discipleship is about selflessly giving our lives for the sake of others, mirroring what Jesus did for us. We have the power to do the same every day of our lives.

Jesus, who bore the curse resulting from humanity's brokenness, sets an example for the future of the church. The very thing we once feared losing—our lives—is now a calling to lay down our lives for others and future generations.

Our children, grandchildren, great-grandchildren, and so on will inherit this responsibility, guided by our example. We need not fear; they will be in good hands as long as we remain faithful to our calling as the church of Jesus Christ. Our role is to help them grasp the significance of the cross—a final act of God that forgives

---

35. Exodus 3:6 (NRSV)

and reconciles our sins, the last step of the covenant. Through the cross, Jesus assumed the curse stemming from humanity's broken covenant, enabling us to trust them with the future of the church. The very thing we once feared losing—our lives—is now entrusted to their care. As long as we faithfully cultivate a culture of covenant hospitality, there is no need for fear. They will be well-equipped to carry this sacred legacy forward.

End of Chapter 2 Summary: Walking in Faith

I will confess that as I wrote this chapter, God took it in a very different direction than I had planned. Like Jacob, I wrestled with God as He spoke the words to my heart, and they flowed to the pages of this chapter. I was blown away by the metaphor of covenant as hospitality. I have been ministering for over twenty years and have never heard or seen it. As I read through the covenant between God and Abram, it became clear to me that if there were a model of hospitality the church must embrace, it is this one.

If there were ever a model to follow on how to demonstrate a culture and a heart of hospitality in our church, it would be the covenant between God and Abraham. Every element is present: love, sacrifice, trust, service, identity, loyalty/faithfulness, shared power, laying down our lives, generosity, and giving away the church to the next generations. Now, we must pray for the God to give us the courage to do it. Lord, help my unbelief; I want to believe.[36]

Principles for Welcoming the Next Generations into a Covenant Relationship

Principle 1: Cultivating Trust through Unconditional Love
In the biblical narrative, trust is foundational to hospitality. Just as God welcomed Abraham into covenant despite his unworthiness, we must extend trust and unconditional love to the next

---

36. Mark 9:24 (NRSV)

generation. Our first call is to love our neighbors as ourselves, embracing those who may have different worldviews and experiences. By modeling holiness and offering unwavering love, we create an environment where trust can flourish.

Principle 2: Sharing Power and Serving Others

To welcome the next generation, we must not only invite their involvement but also genuinely listen to their ideas and concerns. Generosity goes beyond material wealth; it includes giving away our power and resources. As we open our lives and minds to them, we demonstrate humility and a servant's heart. Embracing a culture of hospitality means inviting them into our lives, not just our churches, and being generous with our time and mercy.

Principle 3: Fostering a Family of Belonging

The next generation desires to belong, and we can offer them a spiritual family rooted in covenant hospitality. By pronouncing blessings rather than curses and focusing on what is right in their lives, we show them the love of Christ. Just as God changed Abram's name to Abraham, we invite them to take on the name of Christ and join the family of believers. Self-sacrifice becomes a legacy we pass on, guiding them to carry the torch of faith into the future with confidence.

A Prayer for Walking in Faith

Dear Lord,

We come before You with hearts filled with gratitude for the covenant relationship You initiated with Abraham and embraced us into at Golgotha. We humbly seek Your guidance, Lord, as we embark on a journey to welcome the next generations into this same covenant relationship.

Grant us, O Lord, the wisdom and grace to extend the same boundless love, mercy, and grace to them as You have bestowed upon us. May our hearts be open wide to receive them, making them feel not only welcomed but deeply cherished as members of Your family.

Lord, kindle in us a spirit of curiosity so that we may approach this task with open minds and hearts. Help us recognize that in teaching and mentoring them, there is also much we can learn from their unique perspectives and experiences.

May our efforts, guided by your divine wisdom, cultivate an atmosphere where the next generations find not just a place to belong but a spiritual home where they can flourish and grow in their faith.

In Your holy name, we pray,

Amen.

Reachable Questions for Reflection

1. How is God asking you to lay down your life? What does that look like for your church? What does that look like for you?
2. What are some ways you can foster a culture of hospitality outside the four walls of your church?
3. What are some potential obstacles that might prevent covenant hospitality in your church?
4. On a scale of one to five, how close is your church to embracing a culture of covenant hospitality?

Chapter 3

Embarking into the Unknown
Creating Sacred Spaces and Safe Places

"The Lord is my light and my salvation—
whom shall I fear?"[37]

Fearing the Unknown

Welles and his Mercury Theatre on the Air had adapted H.
G. Wells' *The War of the Worlds* into a phony news bulletin about
a Martian invasion of New Jersey and aired it the night before
Halloween. Many journalists were persuaded that the show had
produced widespread anxiety since some listeners believed the
fake bulletins were the real thing. To his surprise, some listeners
believed the news bulletins were real and called the police, news-
papers, and radio stations in panic. Welles, at only twenty-three
years old, made national headlines the next day after his CBS
show caused widespread alarm.[38]

The natural human reaction is to be afraid of the future. In
ancient biblical times, the sea was a symbol of such dread because
of its mysterious nature. Weather's unpredictability instilled terror
in ancient humans who lacked the knowledge and technology
to foresee it. They invented fantastic tales about strange animals
dwelling in the depths of the ocean. The invention of large
ships and the development of submarines that can investigate

---

37. Psalm 27:11 (NIV)
38. Schwartz, "The Infamous 'War of the Worlds' Radio Broadcast Was
a Magnificent Fluke" (Smithsonian Magazine).

the ocean's depths have given us a newfound confidence in our ability to navigate its waters and reduced the sea's reputation as a place of danger.

In the current day, we are more concerned with the unknowns of space. We have made movies, TV shows, and other forms of entertainment that both feed into and distract from those anxieties. Again, thanks to advances in technology, people are less frightened by space than they once were. Nonetheless, there is still enough of a mystery surrounding space travel and aliens to keep us on our toes.

Dark also tends to represent fear of the unknown. Especially when you're a kid, when alone without the safety of a parent, imaginations can run wild, and minds begin to picture monsters in the closet, creatures under the bed, and monsters overhead. Jesus was well aware of this, which is why he repeatedly taught his contemporaries—and by extension, us—not to be afraid. The antidote to fear is perfect love (1 John 4:18). We feel safer when we have love in our lives. The Jews were paranoid about committing the sin of "uncleanliness," which they associated with things like blood, disease, physical deformities, and refusing to conform to social norms. It is possible to argue that panic led to Jesus' crucifixion. Authorities killed Jesus because they were afraid of the economic and social upheaval that would result from his teachings.

Historically, the church has seemingly been a little double minded. On the one hand, we desperately want to reach out into our communities. The Christian faith has good news to share! We are commissioned to go and make disciples. We were created by God to be His image bearers in the world. Jesus referred to His followers as the "light of the world."[39] Much of the Christian ethos is about being a witness to reach the lost.

Simultaneously, the church's approach to culture has been adversarial. Some well-meaning saints see themselves as pro-

39. Matthew 5:14 (NIV)

tecting the church by demanding conformity from those who enter its sanctuary. Others lament that culture does not reflect Christian values. The result is what has become a colloquialism referred to as the culture war. When I look at Jesus' ministry, the only adversary Jesus ever responded to, even as they sought to undermine Him and ultimately murder Him, was Satan. Wars are used by empires, not the kingdom of God. Adversarial views of those we are seeking to disciple are not helpful. There are those in our culture who view the church with suspicion. They see the church as their enemy instead of messengers with good news. Our purpose as Christians is to reflect the glory of God. We are a light in the darkness. His church becomes the shining city on a hill, and Jesus is the source of light.

Scripture abounds with anecdotes of Jesus' teachings compelling us to love our enemies. The church holds as a key core value and mission, "Go and make disciples of all nations, baptizing them in the name of the Father and of the Son and of the Holy Spirit, and teaching them to obey everything I have commanded you." And then Jesus tags it with the ending, "And surely I am with you always, to the very end of the age."[40] Jesus knew our inclination to fear, so he reminded us that He would be with us.

Throughout his ministry, Jesus crossed the boundaries into what was considered the danger zone of darkness and, in the process, proved we have nothing to fear because perfect love casts out fear. Darkness cannot overcome light. In fact, in the presence of love, hope, and light, the darkness becomes light. Jesus fully understood wars, rumors of wars, and humanity's inclination towards war. By knowing this, His greatest commandment was, "Love the Lord your God with all your heart and with all your soul and with all your mind and with all your strength."[41] He knew it was impossible to love a world in which we were at war.

---

40. Matthew 26:18–19 (NIV)
41. Mark 12:30 (NIV)

It is not only our call to love the world; it is our commission. We do not fear the darkness because Jesus is with us.

Let the Little Children Come to Me

When I was a child, I loved my church. While my mom and dad slept, I would wake up bright and early every Sunday, dress myself, and wait at the end of my driveway for the "Snoopy Bus" to come. The "Snoopy Bus" had Charlie Brown, Snoopy, and the rest of the Peanut Gang painted on the outside of it. Our church bus driver was a milkman, and he always brought chocolate milk and Ding Dongs to all the church bus kids. Once she was old enough, I would dress my little sister, and she waited with me and attended the church. Mr. John would drive, and Mrs. Elaine was the bus mom. She handed out the goodies and handled the discipline. When we boys threatened to get a little out of control, she would quickly rein us in with the threat of a kiss. The last thing an eight-year-old boy like me wanted was a kiss from an "old woman." Mind you, I think she was in her forties, but regardless of how old she was, none of us wanted a kiss from her. Our church was full of surrogate parents and grandparents. My aunt and uncle attended along with their children, but that did not stop me from running the halls, picking fights, and creating chaos. In my defense, I never demanded they essentially feed me sugar intravenously right before church. Despite my hyper-activeness and inability to sit still, my church loved me, and as I have already said, I loved them!

Let Your Light Shine

I was a child of the chaos and darkness. My mom grew up in a religiously oppressive home. She was unable to go to dances, go to football games, wear makeup, or much of anything. For her, Christianity did not represent freedom from the bondage of sin; it meant being enslaved by the rules of the church. She saw a chance to escape and married my father at seventeen. One year later, I was born. Understandably, she wanted nothing to do with the church once she was married and out of the home.

My father's dad was an alcoholic. He was violent, abusive, and unfaithful to his wife. My dad's mother would send my dad to the bars with his father to prevent him from picking up women. After I was grown, my mom told me the story of how my dad awakened one night to his dad standing over him with a knife. He was drunk and was always mean when he was drunk. My dad had to hide outside in the bushes to save his own life. He too was a child of the chaos and darkness.

There was something in my church that was greater than the chaos and darkness trying to threaten innocent children in our community. Almost every Saturday, they would go throughout the community, knock on doors, and leave bubble gum for the kids. When they came to my house, they were deathly afraid of my dad. He worked nights at the rubber plant. It was over 130 degrees in his department almost year-round. He was always seemingly in a grouchy mood unless he was hunting or fishing. If anyone interrupted his sleep during the day, he would roar like Goliath taunting the Israelites, and he was almost as big.

When it came to my house, the canvassers from the church had to be strategic. The driver would wait in a running car. To this day, I am unsure how they determined who would bring the bubble gum to our doorstep. Perhaps they drew straws or took turns. Regardless of who the unlucky person was, they knew to be careful. The driver would not pull into the driveway. They would wait on the street, while the chosen victim would carefully place the bubble gum along with the bus schedule and an invitation to Sunday school on the step. Then he/she would quickly run back to the still-running car and dive into the window as it drove away. I never saw old ladies run as fast as they did when evangelizing my house. Perhaps that is a little bit of an exaggeration, or perhaps it is the mythologized memories of childhood. It is not an exaggeration to say their loving witness had a greater impact than the darkness I witnessed in my home.

From a child's perspective I did not understand the distinction between the chaos of a child's darkness versus that of an adult. I still remember the day I came to the realization that darkness is everywhere, and if we are not careful, we can let our concern for the well-being of those within the church be used by the enemy to keep those who are spiritually unresolved and in need of being discipled out. Remember, fear is not a tool of the kingdom of God. I had been inviting my best friend's parents to church for as long as I can remember. To me, my church was a refuge from the chaos of darkness. It was a sanctuary of safety. I had no inkling it was anything other than that for everyone else. The enemy knew. The principalities of darkness knew. I was too wide-eyed and innocent to see the storm clouds brewing on the horizon. Finally, one day, my friend's parents said yes! I was elated! Sunday came and I paced the halls of the church, awaiting their arrival. I met them in the parking lot. When they walked through the doors of the church, the greeters spoke. It was not long before I saw a flurry of activity from the ushers. They were talking. I still thought nothing about it. I took my seat with the kids on the other side of the church. I saw a couple of ushers talking with them, and then I saw them leave.

My friend's dad worked at a local liquor store at the only mall in town. He did not just work there; he was the manager. As a holiness denomination, we were completely against alcohol. Then we considered it a sin, and church was not the place for sin. If sin were to enter the church, it might contaminate the Christians. Sin brought the chaos of darkness. They never returned to our church. Would you?

I am happy to say they found another church. I am also happy to say that forty-plus years later, my denomination has learned not to fear the chaos of darkness. Having discovered that Jesus drank wine, it was hard to defend the idea that drinking was somehow a sin. We still do not drink alcohol, but today, we acknowledge it because we stand in solidarity with those whose lives, such as my family, have been hurt by alcohol and its effects.

Do Not Worry

"Fear is not real. The only place that fear can exist is in our thoughts of the future. It is a product of our imagination, causing us to fear things that do not at present and may not ever exist."[42]

These words reflect the idea that fear often arises from unfounded worries about the future, and they echo the sentiments of Michel de Montaigne, who, five hundred years ago, observed, "My life has been filled with terrible misfortune, most of which never happened."[43]

A 2015 study revealed 97 percent of the things we worry about are unnecessary.[44] Despite such insights, it appears that humanity has struggled with unnecessary fear for centuries, as similar sentiments were expressed by Jesus over two thousand years ago.

In the realm of spirituality, darkness and chaos need not pose a threat to the institution of the church or to Christians in general. As Psalm 30:5 reminds us, "For his anger lasts only a moment, but his favor lasts a lifetime; weeping may stay for the night, but rejoicing comes in the morning."[45] However, it is worth noting that while the church has made progress, many of those outside the church still perceive it as a place of judgment. Simultaneously, some within the church fear the darkness or "sin" of the world, worrying that it might extinguish or diminish their spiritual light.

Such fears often stem from concerns about compromising values or tolerating sin. Common sayings like "one bad apple spoils the batch" and "A little yeast works through the whole

---

42. *After Earth* (Columbia Pictures, 2013).
43. Goewey, "85 Percent of What We Worry About Never Happens" (Huffpost).
44. Goewey, "85 Percent of What We Worry About Never Happens" (Huffpost).
45. Psalm 30:5 (NIV)

batch of dough" illustrate this concern.[46] Yet, it is crucial to recognize that we are not alone in facing these challenges. When we invite the Holy Spirit into our midst, we are empowered. With the Holy Spirit's guidance and the support of fellow believers, we gain the strength to help others escape the metaphorical pit of darkness. The light within us dispels the darkness. This truth aligns with Jesus' words, "I am the vine; you are the branches. If a man remains in me and I in him, he will bear much fruit; apart from me you can do nothing."[47]

Personally, I do not fear darkness, likely because of God's faithfulness to me during the chaos of my childhood. However, I do take the consequences of embracing darkness seriously, understanding the dangers and harm it can cause. We can address individual issues such as addiction, disease, broken relationships, and broken families, but ultimately, all sins lead to death. Nevertheless, welcoming broken people into our churches does not mean we ignore or normalize their brokenness. Instead, we accept them as they are and love them too much to leave them broken. Once they experience our genuine love, they become open to gentle guidance towards the light of Jesus.

During my youth, I caused chaos within the church community. However, the church did not ignore or normalize my behavior. Instead, they mentored me, modeled better behavior, and, most importantly, offered me unconditional love. They never attempted to cast me out of the church, even when I kicked the pastor once. They continued to send a bus to pick me up, offered me chocolate milk and ding dongs, and eventually, I became a youth leader and began mentoring other teenagers.

In fact, one leader, now in his seventies, credits me, during my youth, for his son's love for the church today. When they were new to the area, and his son was only twelve, I took him under my adolescent wing, introduced him to the town, made

---

46. Galatians 5:9 (NIV)
47. John 15:9 (NIV)

him feel welcome in the church, and modeled for him the love of the Lord that had been shown to me. Today, his son pastors a thriving church with over a thousand members.

Turn Your Eyes Upon Jesus

One of my favorite hymns is "Turn Your Eyes upon Jesus."[48] The lyrics are a powerful reminder that goes with us and will be with us wherever we go.[49] The lyrics are as follows:

Verse 1

O soul are you weary and troubled

No light in the darkness you see

There's light for a look at the Savior

And life more abundant and free

Chorus:

Turn your eyes upon Jesus

Look full in his wonderful face

And the things of earth will grow strangely dim. In the light of his glory and grace

Verse 2

His word shall not fail you he promised

Believe him and all will be well

Then go to a world that is dying

His perfect salvation to tell

---

48. "Turn Your Eyes Upon Jesus" lyrics written by Helen Howarth Lemmel, © Curb Songs, Littleberace Music, Okapione Music, Integrity's Hosanna! Music, New Spring Publishing Inc., Mercy/vineyard Publishing. Public domain.
49. Joshua 1:9 (NIV)

Chorus:

Turn your eyes upon Jesus

Look full in his wonderful face

And the things of earth will grow strangely dim In the light of his glory and grace

Verse 3:

O soul are you weary and troubled

No light in the darkness you see

There's light for a look at the Savior

And life more abundant and free

Chorus:

Turn your eyes upon Jesus

Look full in his wonderful face

And the things of earth will grow strangely dim In the light of his glory and grace.[50]

Guardians of Faith: Nurturing the Future Amidst Modern Challenges

This song reminds me of the story of ancient Byzantine monks who adopted a sacred practice as a reminder of God's promise that He is with us. The Church of the Nativity is located in the ancient Palestinian city of Bethlehem. This historic church, now belonging to the Eastern Orthodox tradition, proudly claims to be the world's oldest Christian church. Its origins can be traced back to a commission by Constantine the Great, following a visit by his mother Helena to Jerusalem and Bethlehem in 325–326. The church's construction likely began between 330 and 333, with its dedication taking place on May 31, 339.

---

50. "Turn Your Eyes Upon Jesus" lyrics written by Helen Howarth Lemmel, © Curb Songs, Littleberace Music, Okapione Music, Integrity's Hosanna! Music, New Spring Publishing Inc., Mercy/vineyard Publishing. Public domain.

Subsequently, Byzantine Emperor Justinian (reigned 527–565) oversaw the construction of a new basilica, which included the addition of a porch or narthex and the replacement of the original octagonal sanctuary with a cruciform transept featuring three apses. Despite these alterations, the building's fundamental character, including its atrium and a basilica with a central nave and four side aisles, remained largely intact.[51]

In the sacred tradition of The Church of the Nativity and many other Eastern Christian Orthodox churches, a striking custom involves the use of ornately decorated ostrich eggs suspended from the church's ceiling. These eggs are adorned with intricate designs in gold, silver, and various colors, some even transformed into light fixtures or hinged containers with icons inside. This practice holds deep significance and has its roots in a story associated with the ostrich.[52]

The ostrich, despite being one of the largest birds, faces a unique challenge due to its relatively small brain in proportion to its large eyes. When an ostrich lays its eggs, it must bury them in the sand, not just as mere snacks but as essential sustenance for potential predators lurking nearby. To protect its future offspring, the ostrich carefully conceals the eggs in a nondescript location and covers them to prevent discovery by predators.

However, the ostrich encounters a peculiar dilemma—the tendency to forget the precise location of its hidden eggs. Over time, the ostrich has learned a critical lesson: it can never divert its attention entirely from its eggs. Despite its capacity to roam and explore, it must always maintain one eye on those concealed, invisible eggs. Losing sight of the egg means forfeiting its future, its descendants, and its hope.

---

51. Church of the Nativity—Wikipedia. "Church of the Nativity—Wikipedia," July 5, 2017. https://en.wikipedia.org/wiki/Church_of_the_Nativity.

52. "مجلة الاتحاد العام للآثاريين العرب (١٥)," Journal of the General Union of Arab Archaeologists 15 (2014): 23-41

This poignant story and the symbolic use of ostrich eggs serve as a powerful reminder of the need for unwavering vigilance and protection of what is most precious to us. Just as the ostrich must guard its hidden eggs with unwavering focus, we too must cherish and protect the invaluable aspects of our lives to ensure a bright and secure future.

As people of faith, one of our profound concerns is the potential loss of our children to the influences of the world, which is especially relevant in our present times. A quick glance at recent national news headlines underscores the concerning forces at play. There are distressing efforts to introduce sexualization to our children at an early age. In some educational settings, the emphasis appears to be on teaching young children about pronouns even before they can fully grasp reading. Notably, American Girl has even introduced a book accompanying their dolls, which imparts information about gender changes to young girls.[53] The infiltration of drugs into classrooms is becoming an alarming concern. Some drug dealers are resorting to tactics that involve disguising drugs to resemble candy, further exacerbating the issue.[54]

Shalom as the Pathway to Peace and Wholeness

During my childhood, my church in the small, seemingly insignificant city of Holt, Alabama, organized a children's choir, and I was overjoyed at the opportunity to participate. I thoroughly enjoyed standing on the stage, singing alongside other children, and occasionally taking on solo roles. My appeal as a soloist may not have been solely due to my singing abilities but rather because I provided entertaining unpredictability. As a hyperactive,

---

53. Keane, Isabel. "Title of the Article." New York Post, December 7, 2022, https://nypost.com/2022/12/07/american-girl-angers-parents-with-book-teaching-kids-about-gender-expression/#

54. Madison Weil, "12,000 Fentanyl Pills Hidden Inside Popular Candy Packaging," 10News, posted October 21, 2022, https://www.10news.com/news/local-news/12-000-fentanyl-pills-hidden-inside-popular-candy-packaging.

ADHD, outgoing child with an energetic personality, I often engaged in various antics. "Down in My Heart" was among my cherished songs, whose chorus I would jubilantly sing at the top of my lungs.[55] The chorus goes:

I've got the peace that passes understanding Down in my heart, (where?) Down in my heart, (where?) Down in my heart, I've got the peace that passes understanding Down in my heart, (where?) Down in my heart to stay.[56]

I misunderstood the lyrics of that song, and at the tender age of six, no one corrected me. I believed the lyrics were, "I have the pissy, passy understanding down in my heart." I had little comprehension of the "peace that passes understanding," so "pissy" or "passy" seemed just as relevant and meaningful. It wasn't until my adolescent years that I realized I had been singing those words incorrectly.

In a similar vein, we sometimes misinterpret the Hebrew word "Shalom." While it means peace, it doesn't imply the absence of conflict. For those who have been Christians for a while, beyond the initial euphoria of experiencing grace, they understand that surrendering our way to follow Jesus can lead to significant conflict. Just ask someone who has converted from Islam to Christianity. Shalom means wholeness and completeness. It's the inner peace that stems from the knowledge that, despite the chaos swirling around us and the "monsters" we may encounter in the darkness, God's love will sustain us. In essence, it's the "peace that passes understanding" residing deep in our hearts, and if we follow and trust Jesus, it's there to stay.

---

55. "Down in My Heart." Traditional Christian Children's Song, attributed to George Willis Cooke. Public domain.
56. "Down in My Heart." Traditional Christian Children's Song, attributed to George Willis Cooke. Public domain.

Learning to Walk in the Dark

Barbara Brown Taylor is an American author, Episcopal priest, and theologian known for her books on spirituality, faith, and religion. In her book *Learning to Walk in the Dark,* she explores the idea of embracing darkness in our lives, both metaphorically and literally. She encourages readers to confront and learn from the various "dark" experiences and periods in life, which can include times of uncertainty, doubt, suffering, and the unknown. Through her writing, she suggests that these dark moments can be opportunities for growth, transformation, and deeper spiritual understanding. The book invites readers to consider the value of darkness and to find meaning and wisdom in it.

She writes, "Darkness is shorthand for anything that scares me—either because I am sure that I do not have the resources to survive it or because I do not want to find out."[57] When we are told to go out into the darkness, it is easy to become distracted by the enemy, who will tempt us to remain in the safety of the sanctuary. Perhaps these fears will help us to have a little more grace for the disciples, post-crucifixion, who lived in fear for their lives? This story, along with Jesus' teaching and example, is we do not fear the darkness. If we always keep our eyes on Christ, darkness has no power over us or our children. However, the moral of this story reminds us: if we keep our eyes on Jesus, we can have hope that we will not forfeit the future, lose hope, and lose our children.

This narrative, coupled with Jesus' teachings and actions, reminds us that we need not fear the darkness. As long as we keep our eyes fixed upon our risen savior who conquered fear and death, darkness holds no sway over us or our children. Nonetheless, the moral of this tale serves as a reminder: by keeping our eyes on Jesus, we can nurture hope and safeguard our future, preventing

---

57. Barbara Brown Taylor, *Learning to Walk in the Dark* (San Francisco: HarperOne, 2014).

its forfeiture and protecting our children. Once more, Taylor offers us guidance, stating, "When the lights go out in your life, God does not leave the building. Instead, God goes looking for you."[58]

While our divine mission calls us to step into the darkness, we don't embark without a plan. Our strategy is to bring the good news. As we step forward, we should emulate Jesus, who reserved His sternest rebukes for the religious elite but extended grace and hospitality to those branded as "unclean" by the religious establishment. Evangelism is no walk in the park; it demands keen discernment. Many of us engaged in sharing the good news have been endowed with the spiritual gift of mercy, a gift that can easily be exploited. We are compassionate souls, yet we must also embody the wisdom of serpents and the innocence of doves. Such discernment arises from an intimate connection with the Lord.

Amid this caution, there's a crucial reminder: our duty isn't to save or rescue those who remain spiritually unresolved. We are not God. We are like John the Baptist. A "voice crying in the wilderness."[59] We must navigate the tension known as the "via media" or middle way, as articulated by John Wesley.[60] In this tension, some insist that specific behaviors must be adhered to for salvation. On the other side, critics of legalism argue for grace and cite Jesus' compassion for Gentiles, the infirm, the blind, the woman at the well, the leper, and others whom society considered unclean or unworthy.

The middle way is marked by mercy; it meets people where they are and as they are but loves them too much to leave them unchanged. Hence, the good news we share conveys that Jesus died on the cross to atone for their sins, but they must repent. Repentance isn't merely an admission of wrongdoing; it signifies

---

58. Barbara Brown Taylor, *Learning to Walk in the Dark* (San Francisco: HarperOne, 2014).
59. Mark 1:3, NIV.
60. Watts, Joel. "Was Wesley Against the Middle Way?" United Methodist Insight.

a complete turn from living by one's own standards to selflessly following Jesus' example. It entails living with consideration for others and their well-being. As we navigate this tension, let's remind ourselves that Jesus was crucified between two criminals. We might face crucifixion, but a sacrifice devoid of consequences isn't truly a sacrifice at all.

Extending Grace Across Generations

When tension arises, it's common for the church to turn inward, with members sometimes engaging in conflicts among themselves. It's important to extend grace to those within the church who fear the darkness, just as we do for those who remain spiritually unresolved. Many of these individuals were stalwarts of the faith from generations past, and we must consider the significant changes they have experienced. For them, it may feel like the ground is shifting beneath their feet.

Young seminarians often graduate with hearts filled with knowledge and expansive visions, eager to implement everything they've learned. However, they frequently encounter challenges in their initial assignments because they fail to adjust their approach to fit the context of their local congregations. It's crucial to remember that their congregations haven't spent the past four or five years immersed in the world of academia. Neglecting this reality can lead to painful experiences for both the seminarians and their congregations if these tensions aren't navigated with compassion.

As someone who coaches and counsels pastors, I often hear that conflicts have arisen within congregations, leaving pastors perplexed about the reasons behind them. Unfortunately, by the time these conflicts reach me, sides have often been chosen, and the church is in crisis. I've witnessed numerous young and idealistic pastors leave the ministry due to such experiences, and many churches face closure or significant distress as a result. My point is to be patient with those outside the church but make your shift intentionally. Almost always, I find the pastor has no clear and compelling vision that has been communicated to the church. Cast a clear and compelling vision, and the older generation will follow you to the ends of the earth. Additionally, please do not wait until you and or your church are in crisis before you seek the wisdom of a mentor or find a pastoral coach such as me or a denominational leader.

I previously mentioned that my mother grew up in a spiritually oppressive home. I also shared that my home church ousted my best friend's parents because his father worked at a liquor store in the mall. The same man who was exceedingly legalistic with my mother showed remarkable compassion toward those he referred to as "the lost." He had only completed third grade, hailed from a family of nineteen children, and all the boys were tasked with farm work instead of attending school. My grandmother taught him to read using the Bible. From our educated vantage point, he appeared oppressive, but from his perspective, he was safeguarding my mother.

Years later, my mother would find Jesus at the same church that had expelled my best friend's parents. That church would mentor and equip her for youth ministry. Interestingly, the same spiritually oppressive grandfather would play a pivotal role in my father's salvation. My father would eventually surrender his life to God, heed a call to ministry, quit a well-paying job at B.F. Goodrich, and relocate our family 300 miles north to Nashville, Tennessee.

When my family moved to Nashville for my father to commence his studies, it was an act of faith. Neither my father nor my mother had secured jobs beforehand; they trusted that God would provide. Just one week after our arrival in Nashville, my father landed a job at UPS. A few weeks later, my mother found work as a cosmetologist. Despite living below the poverty line while my father completed his education, we never went hungry. It's easy to criticize both my grandfather's legalism and my home church from one perspective, but even in their flawed state, God still used them. As we venture into the darkness, we may not always agree on the methods, and we are all broken vessels, but God transcends our men and methods as well as the darkness that seems to encroach upon our safe spaces.

We also refrain from offering false hope. Jesus' message revolved around the offer of living water, assuring that those who partook of His living water would never thirst again. He extended the shalom of God, a peace that transcends the mere absence of external conflicts, chaos, or turmoil; rather, it signifies a state of wholeness, an inner peace. Yet, it's crucial to acknowledge that salvation is an ongoing journey, not a one-time event. God is perpetually in the process of saving us, and we must continually choose to follow His path. Throughout this journey, we will encounter both good and bad days, but as we increasingly walk in the footsteps of Jesus, this path becomes more familiar.

Some mistakenly conflate inner peace with an illusion of the absence of darkness and chaos. Even after embracing Jesus as our Savior, the turbulence of a fallen world persists. As Christians, we still grapple with troubles and occasionally find ourselves dealing with brokenness, whether it be anxiety or financial struggles. Following our decision to follow Jesus, our bank accounts don't magically fill with abundance. Those grappling with addiction must continue their arduous path to recovery, and individuals bearing emotional wounds may find benefit in the counsel of both the Holy Spirit and professional therapists.

Once again, Jesus' narrative underscores the reality of the life we are called to lead. As I pen this chapter, the spirit of Christmas fills the air during the Advent season. Our towns are adorned with tinsel, chestnuts roast over open fires, and neighbors adorn their homes with nativity scenes and radiant Christmas lights illuminating the night. Yet, amidst these signs of hope, our nation grapples with profound division. Dominating the news is the story of a Satanic temple in one town demanding the placement of a satanic nativity alongside the Christian nativity, further accentuating the contrasts within our society.[61] But God! The presence of God through the indwelling of the Holy Spirit changes the story from chaos to peace.

Old Creation Narratives

One of my favorite books of the Bible is Genesis. Our creation story is so different than any other narrative that existed at the time. While we inside the church get bogged down arguing the (false) contention between religion and science for literal seven days of creation versus evolution, we miss the hope in this story. You may recall my section about biblical exegesis and how we must consider the original context and try to read the scripture from the perspective of the original intended audience. Genesis is a prime example of the jubilant hope that is found when we immerse ourselves in the scripture instead of a flat literal reading,

The Enuma Elish is a Mesopotamian myth that describes the creation of the world and the rise of the gods.[62] In this narrative, the world begins as a watery abyss called the "Apsu," representing the sweet, fresh waters, and "Tiamat," representing the salty, chaotic waters.

The story begins with the god Apsu and the goddess Tiamat, who are the primordial beings representing these watery elements. They give birth to the first generation of gods, known as the "Elder Gods."[63] However, these younger gods are noisy and disturb Apsu's rest. Apsu decides to destroy them, but one of the younger

---

61. Adams, Andrew. "Satanic Temple to Install Sol Invictus Holiday Display at State Capitol Rotunda." State Journal-Register. Published December 18, 2022. Accessed April 13, 2023. https://www.sj-r.com/story/news/state/2021/12/18/satanic-temple-install-holiday-display-illinois-state-capitol/8952418002/.
62. *Enuma Elish—The Babylonian Epic of Creation*, translated by L.W. King, accessed May 25, 2023, http://www.sacred-texts.com/ane/enuma.htm.
63. *Enuma Elish—The Babylonian Epic of Creation*, translated by L.W. King, accessed September 25, 2023, http://www.sacred-texts.com/ane/enuma.htm.

gods, Ea (also known as Enki), learns of the plan and kills Apsu to protect the others.[64]

Tiamat, enraged by the death of Apsu, becomes the primary antagonist in the narrative. She creates an army of monstrous creatures and appoints the god Kingu as her new consort and leader of the forces. Tiamat seeks revenge on Ea and the younger gods for Apsu's death.

The gods, led by the god Marduk, choose him as their champion to confront Tiamat and her forces. Marduk offers to defeat Tiamat in exchange for being made the chief of the gods, and the other gods agree. In a great battle, Marduk defeats Tiamat, splitting her into two halves, and creates the heavens and the earth from her remains.

Marduk goes on to establish order in the universe, assigning roles to the gods and creating humanity from the blood of Kingu. The Enuma Elish is often seen as a narrative that celebrates the victory of order and civilization over chaos and represents the divine authority of Marduk as the chief god of the Babylonian pantheon.

The profound disparity between this chaotic narrative and the Genesis account, which avoids becoming ensnared in a convoluted web of chaos and conflict, never fails to inspire me. Genesis presents a God who refrains from engaging in power struggles with other deities, choosing instead to step into a world characterized by formlessness and chaos. With the mere resonance of His voice, He ushers in peace, reminiscent of Jesus calming the turbulent waters of a storm.[65] Genesis narrates the creation of humanity in the divine image, emphasizing a foundation built on relationship and love, with God breathing life into our very beings. Reflecting on God's remarkable ability to bring tranquility to a shapeless Earth through His voice and to breathe life into clay, one can

---

64. *Enuma Elish—The Babylonian Epic of Creation*, translated by L.W. King, accessed September 25, 2023, http://www.sacred-texts.com/ane/enuma.htm.
65. Gospel of Mark 4:35–41 (NIV)

only imagine the profound transformative power of His Spirit when we extend an invitation for Him to "tabernacle" within us. As children of God, we need not dwell in the shadow of a chaotic creation story; ours is a narrative of shalom.[66]

A Not-So-Silent Night

We have greatly romanticized the story of Jesus' birth. Our manger scenes, while beautiful, do not depict the horrific and harsh conditions, the chaos, and the dark world into which this child was born. We love to depict the world into which Jesus was born and thus the Christmas season as merry and bright, but the world was very much messy and broken. The night of Jesus birther was far from a "silent night." Let's remove the varnish and polish we have applied to the first Christmas story.

When Mary received the angel's message of her impending motherhood, her heart overflowed with joy.[67] Yet, in the harsh realm of earthly consequences, a woman found unfaithful to her betrothed could face dire punishment, even death. Joseph, her betrothed, had to summon an extraordinary measure of faith to embrace the angel's words and defy the gravitational pull of tradition and societal norms. Back then, Jewish tradition held no inkling of the Messiah's arrival through a virgin birth; the community had no framework for accepting Mary's remarkable claim. Her life must have been fraught with tension and uncertainty.

Going beyond the initial astonishment, Mary and Joseph received more earthbound news, delivered not by angels but through a human messenger. There were no angelic choruses or cosmic fanfare—just the announcement that Caesar Augustus had ordered a census.[68] This decree forced Mary and Joseph into a daunting ninety-mile journey to Bethlehem, with Mary in her third trimester. It's hard to fathom a third-trimester pregnant

---

66. Romans 8:9–11 (NIV)
67. Luke 1:26–38 (NIV)
68. Luke 2:1–5 (NIV)

woman, let alone a young girl of thirteen, riding a donkey on such a journey.

Once they arrived in Bethlehem, it appeared Joseph was a stereotypical man and failed to secure reservations prior to their arrival. Thus, there was no room, and she was forced to give birth in an animal's stable. The Creator of the universe made His earthly debut in a humble feeding trough. Fast forward a few years, and the Magi arrived. Recognizing the child's extraordinary significance, they brought gifts befitting a king. Perhaps this is finally a hint of merry and bright during the messy and broken.

However, not long after, another heavenly messenger appeared to Joseph in a dream with a critical message: "Get up, take the child and His mother, and flee to Egypt, and stay there until I tell you, for Herod intends to search for the child to destroy Him."[69]

If we were unaware of the rest of the story, we might be inclined to think, "They'll have quite a challenge on their hands when He grows up!" However, as we follow Jesus' life and discover, or reaffirm, that they weren't in trouble. They didn't fear Him, even after His true identity was revealed. It was the leaders of the day who feared His message of universal good news, leading to His crucifixion.

If there was anyone who deserved a life devoid of darkness and chaos, it was Jesus. Yet, after His death, we are told that He descended into the ultimate darkness—hell—where He preached the good news. Not even the tumultuous abyss of hell could imprison those who sought to follow the light of the world. The good news is that once we become Christians, darkness and chaos are vanquished, never to return. It doesn't mean we won't experience sickness or pain again. One day, when God's kingdom is fully realized, there will be no more tears or suffering. But until then, we carry the same invitation as the woman at the well: "Come and see the man who told me everything I have ever done." Come and behold the One who loves us despite our sins, who doesn't

---

69. Matthew 2:13–15 (NIV)

shame us but offers a way out of the darkness. The world may not suddenly be at peace, but in the proximity of Jesus, there is peace. As Jesus puts it, "I have told you these things, so that in me you may have peace. In this world you will have trouble. But take heart! I have overcome the world."[70]

Sacred Spaces in Dark Places

As we go into the unknown, we can create sacred spaces, even in dark places. No matter the circumstance, we never cede ground to the enemy. Jesus told Peter, "Upon this rock I shall build my church and the gates of Hades will not overcome it."[71] Some context behind this scripture gives some powerful clarification to the truth of this scripture and thus has strong implications for us as we go into the darkness. After Peter proclaimed Jesus to be the Christ, the Son of the Living God, Jesus now addresses Peter's claim. Insisting that God the Father was responsible for Peter's insight, Jesus proclaimed Peter blessed for having realized this.

There's some clever play on words going on here. Peter's name in Greek, Petros, literally means "a rock" or "a stone," and the term Jesus uses for the base, Petra, indicates "rock" in the sense of substance or material.[72] Neither "you are Petros and on this Petros I will build…" nor "you are Petra and on this Petra, I will build…" are statements made by Jesus. Instead, He identifies you as a rock, or Petra, and declares, "Upon this rock I will build my church."[73] What Peter has just spoken is that Jesus is "the Christ, the Son of the living God," the foundation on which God will build His church.[74] It was not the literal rock nor Peter that Jesus

---

70. John 16:3 (NIV)

71. Matthew 16:18 (NIV)

72. s Rachelle Starr, *Outrageous Obedience: Answering God's Call to Shine in the Darkest Places* (Bloomington, MN: Bethany House Publishers, November 8, 2022).

73. Matthew 16:18, NIV.

74. Matthew 16:18, NIV.

was declaring to have the power to go on offense against the gates of hell; it was Peter's confession that Jesus was the Son of God.

At that significant moment of confession, Jesus and His disciples found themselves in Caesarea Philippi, a place known for its pagan worship centered around a cave dedicated to the god Pan. It's interesting to note that from where they were standing, they could see the very rock where the grotto of Pan had been carved out.[75] This cave had a notorious reputation among the Jews due to its rumored bottomless pit and its association with disturbing practices like infanticide and bestiality.[76] So, when Jesus declared that the forces of hell would not prevail against the impending advance of the kingdom of God, it was as if they were gazing into the depths of that dark abyss, fully aware of the darkness they were up against.

Embracing the Call to Shine Light in Dark Places

I can think of a couple of real-life examples of the church going into the darkness and attacking the gates of hell. The first story comes from a lady named Rachelle. Inspired by the biblical story of Esther, she prayed to the Lord, "Whatever you want to use me for, I'm here."[77] She began thinking of Esther's scarlet-colored rope on her robe. Then she thought about that word, "scarlet." But then she also felt the Lord telling her to get to work—this week, today, right now!

Sometime later, Rachelle found herself in a strip club with a young woman who was looking for work to feed her five children. She had been drinking all day to silence the shame of taking her clothes off for strangers. And then, after getting some food, she

75. R. T. France, *The Gospel of Matthew* (William B. Eerdmans Publishing Company, 2007).

76. R. T. France, *The Gospel of Matthew* (William B. Eerdmans Publishing Company, 2007).

77. Rachelle Starr, *Outrageous Obedience: Answering God's Call to Shine in the Darkest Places* (Bloomington, MN: Bethany House Publishers, November 8, 2022).

immediately vomited all over Rachelle. Rachelle continued to serve and love this woman despite the vomit, embarrassment, and club owner's rebuke. As Rachelle shared the love of Christ with her, this woman gave her life to Jesus and fell to her knees in prayer. After praying, the woman exclaimed in joy, "I just met Jesus here!"

As the woman began to leave the strip club with the outrageous love of God now burning in her heart, Rachelle asked for her name. The woman replied, "My name is Scarlet." This encounter was made possible because Rachelle was obedient and did not fear the darkness. In fact, she eventually gets permission to begin bringing home-cooked meals into the club for the strippers. This eventually birthed into the ministry named "Scarlet Hope." Because Rachelle did not fear the darkness, she was able to go in and lead someone out of the darkness. Her ministry continues.[78]

While God will sometimes call us into dark places such as strip clubs, often it is in our everyday lives that we have unexpected encounters with people who are lost in the darkness. Tony Compolo tells the following story of an encounter he had in a random café in Hawaii at 3:30 a.m. in his book *The Kingdom of God Is a Party*:[79]

> Up a side street, I found a little place that was still open. I went in, took a seat on one of the stools at the counter, and waited to be served. This was one of those sleazy places that deserves the name "greasy spoon." I did not even touch the menu. I was afraid that if I opened the thing, something gruesome would crawl out. But it was the only place I could find. The fat guy behind the counter came over and asked me, "What d'ya want?"

78. Rachelle Starr, *Outrageous Obedience: Answering God's Call to Shine in the Darkest Places* (Bloomington, MN: Bethany House Publishers, November 8, 2022).
79. Tony Campolo, *The Kingdom of God Is a Party*.

I said I wanted a cup of coffee and a donut. He poured a cup of coffee, wiped his grimy hand on his smudged apron, and then he grabbed a donut off the shelf behind him. I'm a realist. I know that in the back room of that restaurant, donuts are probably dropped on the floor and kicked around. But when everything was out front where I could see it, I really would have appreciated it if he had used a pair of tongs and placed the donut on some wax paper.

As I sat there munching on my donut and sipping my coffee at 3:30 in the morning, the door of the diner suddenly swung open and, to my discomfort, in marched eight or nine provocative and boisterous prostitutes. It was a small place, and they sat on either side of me. Their talk was loud and crude. I felt completely out of place and was just about to make my getaway when I overheard the woman beside me say, "Tomorrow's my birthday. I'm going to be 39."

Her "friend" responded in a nasty tone, "So what do you want from me? A birthday party? What do you want? Ya want me to get you a cake and sing 'Happy Birthday'?" "Come on," said the woman sitting next to me. "Why do you have to be so mean? I was just telling you, that's all. Why do you have to put me down? I was just telling you it was my birthday. I don't want anything from you. I mean, why should you give me a birthday party? I've never had a birthday party in my whole life. Why should I have one now?"

When I heard that, I made a decision. I sat and waited until the women had left. Then I called over the fat guy behind the counter, and I asked him, "Do they come in here every night?" "Yeah!" he answered. "The one right next to me, does she come here every night?" "Yeah!" he said. "That's Agnes. Yeah, she comes in here every night. Why d'ya wanta know?" "Because I heard her say that tomorrow is her birthday," I told him. "What do you say you and I do something about that? What do you think about us throwing a birthday party for her—right here—tomorrow night?"

A cute smile slowly crossed his chubby cheeks, and he answered with measured delight, "That's great! I like it! That's a great idea!" Calling to his wife, who did the cooking in the back room, he shouted, "Hey! Come out here! This guy's got a great idea. Tomorrow's Agnes's birthday. This guy wants us to go in with him and throw a birthday party for her—right here—tomorrow night!"

His wife came out of the back room all bright and smiley. She said, "That's wonderful! You know Agnes is one of those people who is really nice and kind, and nobody does anything nice and kind for her."

"Look," I told them, "if it's okay with you, I'll get back here tomorrow morning at about 2:30 and decorate the place. I'll even get a birthday cake!" "No way," said Harry (that was his name). "The birthday cake's my thing. I'll make the cake."

At 2:30 the next morning, I was back at the diner. I had picked up some crepe-paper decorations at the store and had made a sign out of big pieces of cardboard that read, "Happy Birthday, Agnes!" I decorated the diner from one end to the other. I had that diner looking good.

The woman who did the cooking must have gotten the word out on the street because by 3:15, every prostitute in Honolulu was in the place. It was wall-to-wall prostitutes and me! At 3:30 on the dot, the door of the diner swung open, and in came Agnes and her friend. I had everybody ready (after all, I was kind of the M.C. of the affair), and when they came in, we all screamed, "Happy birthday!"

Never have I seen a person so flabbergasted, so stunned, so shaken. Her mouth fell open. Her legs seemed to buckle a bit. Her friend grabbed her arm to steady her. As she was led to sit on one of the stools along the counter, we all sang "Happy Birthday" to her.

As we came to the end of our singing with "Happy birthday, dear Agnes, happy birthday to you," her eyes moistened. Then, when the birthday cake with all the candles on it was carried out, she lost it and just openly cried.

Harry gruffly mumbled, "Blow out the candles, Agnes! Come on! Blow out the candles! If you don't blow out the candles,

I'm gonna hafta blow out the candles." And, after an endless few seconds, he did. Then he handed her a knife and told her, "Cut the cake, Agnes. Yo, Agnes, we all want some cake."

Agnes looked down at the cake. Then, without taking her eyes off it, she slowly and softly said, "Look, Harry, is it all right with you if; I mean, is it okay if I kind of what I want to ask you is; is it O.K. if I keep the cake a little while? I mean, is it all right if we don't eat it right away?"

Harry shrugged and answered, "Sure! It's O.K. If you want to keep the cake, keep the cake. Take it home if you want to." "Can I?" she asked. Then, looking at me, she said, "I live just down the street a couple of doors. I want to take the cake home, okay? I'll be right back. Honest!" She got off the stool, picked up the cake, and carrying it like it was the Holy Grail, walked slowly toward the door. As we all just stood there motionless, she left.

When the door closed, there was a stunned silence in the place. Not knowing what else to do, I broke the silence by saying, "What do you say we pray?"

Looking back on it now, it seems more than strange for a sociologist to be leading a prayer meeting with a bunch of prostitutes in a diner in Honolulu at 3:30 in the morning. But then it just felt like the right thing to do. I prayed for Agnes. I prayed for her salvation. I prayed that her life would be changed and that God would be good to her.

When I finished, Harry leaned over the counter, and with a trace of hostility in his voice, he said, "Hey! You never told me you were a preacher. What kind of church do you belong to?" In one of those moments when just the right words came, I answered, "I belong to a church that throws birthday parties for prostitutes at 3:30 in the morning."

Harry waited a moment and then almost sneered as he answered, "No, you don't. There's no church like that. If there was, I'd join it. I'd join a church like that!"

Wouldn't we all? Wouldn't we all like to join a church that throws birthday parties for prostitutes at 3:30 in the morning? Well, that's the kind of church that Jesus came to create!

End of Chapter 3 Summary: Embarking into the Unknown

We need not fear the darkness or the chaos, whether it is a strip club, a prostitute, or someone or something we perceive as toxic people and culture or even pure evil. Our call as the people of God is to enter the darkness but to always keep our eyes on the resurrected Jesus. His presence is our peace. Jesus talked to Samaritan women, healed lepers, and made the lame walk and the blind see on the Sabbath. He even touched blood. He broke all the rules, and we crucified Him for it. We had the opportunity to save Him but got caught up in the emotion of the crowd and chose to save a sinner and kill our savior. But before we fall into despair, we must also remember Jesus' dying words, "Father, forgive them, they know not what they do."[80]

As I reflect on our call into the unknown and to penetrate the darkness with light, I am reminded that courage is not the absence of fear; it is trusting, despite the fear, that things will be okay. The Celtic people believed there were "thin places" between heaven and earth.[81] The places might be mountain tops or other physical places that held special meaning.

Richard Rhor calls this place "the edge" and suggests we should cultivate being there. "The edge is a holy place, or as the Celts called it, 'a thin place' and you have to be taught how to live there. To take your position on the spiritual edge of things is to learn how to move safely in and out, back, and forth, across and return." The reality is when heaven and earth meet, a thin place is discovered.

---

80. Luke 23:34 (KJV)
81. Phillips, "Richard Rohr—The Celts Didn't Invent Thin Places."

Principles for Creating Sacred Spaces and Safe Places

Principle 1: Embrace the Darkness with Shalom

In our Christian journey, we must remember the true meaning of "Shalom." It signifies wholeness and completeness, not just the absence of conflict. To create sacred spaces, we must embrace the darkness in people's lives and offer the inner peace that comes from trusting in God's sustaining love. Just as Jesus didn't fear the darkness but brought hope, we too should enter challenging circumstances with grace and hope, knowing that God goes looking for us when the lights go out. Sacred spaces begin with recognizing the chaos and offering God's peace.

Principle 2: The Via Media of Mercy

In navigating the tensions within the Christian community, we should follow the "via media," as articulated by John Wesley. This middle way is marked by mercy, meeting people where they are but loving them too much to leave them unchanged. Safe spaces are places where judgment is replaced by understanding and compassion. We must convey the good news of Jesus' sacrifice for sin, but also emphasize the importance of repentance, a turn from living by our own standards to selflessly following Jesus. Safe spaces are characterized by grace, acceptance, and the transformative power of Christ's love.

Principle 3: Be the Light in the Darkness

Creating sacred spaces often means stepping into the darkness, just as Jesus did. We should follow His example of extending grace and hospitality to those in need, even in unexpected places. Whether it's ministering in a strip club or a late-night diner, our mission is to be a light in dark places. Safe spaces are where people find unexpected love, kindness, and acceptance. Like the church that threw a birthday party for Agnes at 3:30 in the morning, we should be willing to go to unconventional places and demonstrate God's unconditional love.

A Prayer for Embarking into the Unknown, Creating Safe Spaces, and Sharing Sacred Spaces

Lord, we recognize that Gen Z is often described as the "most anxious generation." It comes as no surprise in an age where we find ourselves drowning in an overwhelming sea of information, making it challenging to discern the vital voices amidst the cacophony of noise.

In a world where fear is wielded as a currency by empires and leaders who employ deception to sow confusion, grant us the courage to step boldly into the darkness. May we shine Your radiant light as a beacon of hope, piercing through the shadows of uncertainty. Let our words be imbued with Your boundless love, echoing the very words that Jesus spoke to calm the tumultuous sea, saying, "Peace, be still."

Lord, instill in us the audacity to emulate the sentiments expressed by Saint Francis in his timeless prayer:

"Lord, make me an instrument of your peace:
where there is hatred, let me sow love;
where there is injury, grant me the capacity to pardon;
where there is doubt, nurture within me unwavering faith;
where there is despair, kindle the flame of hope;
where there is darkness, illuminate with your divine light;
where there is sadness, infuse the spirit with abiding joy."

We offer this prayer in earnest, trusting in Your grace and guidance.

Amen.

Reachable Questions for Reflection

1. Describe to the group a time when you were afraid of the darkness and chaos, but God surprised you.
2. What are some current fears you may be experiencing where you need God to remind you that His light dispels the darkness?

3. Is there someone in your life God is calling you to see through His eyes in order to offer grace?
4. What are some areas of the unknown or "places of darkness" that God may be calling you and your church to enter in with your light?
5. What are some thin places in your life? In your community?

Chapter 4

Leading by Example
Building Bridges to Culture and Community

"Therefore, if anyone is in Christ, the new creation has come: The old has gone, the new is here!" [82]

Digging Deep Wells

A few years ago, I was attending a regional gathering for the Church of the Nazarene, and Dr. T. Scott Daniels shared an of-ten-repeated story about an American rancher and sheepherder who got the chance to spend time with other ranchers and sheepherders in the outback of Australia and New Zealand. The rancher noticed quickly that they didn't have many fences keeping the herd or the flock in place. When he asked about it, the herders from down under remarked, "We learned decades ago that if you dig really good and deep wells, the sheep and cattle won't wander from them, and you don't need as many fences." In these very divisive times, both inside and outside the church, I have grown to love that simple illustration and return to it often to think about how we might work for unity within the very diverse Body of Christ. [83]

When I heard that story, it resonated with me and has contin-ued to echo in the far reaches of my conscious and subconscious mind for ten years. I have tried to think about how the body of Christ lives this out in practical ways with questions such as, "What

---

82. 2 Corinthians 2:15 (NIV)
83. Mark D. Baker, *Centered Set Church: Embracing a Paradigm Shift in Ministry*, 2nd ed. (Abingdon Press, 2021), Kindle edition.

do deep wells look like?" "What does discipleship look like?" "How does one measure Christian maturity in such a context?" Further research led me to Mark D. Baker's book *Centered Set Church*.[84] He and others helped me answer these questions and more.

Deep wells consist of fresh water. In the context of reaching and discipling the next generations, the deep water consists of the unconditional love of God. It is unfortunate, but the love of God, like discipleship, has become sort of an esoteric phrase for the church. Everyone has an idea of what it means, but without defining specifics and real-life examples, they are not likely to be lived out in consistent ways and will not be reproducible or scalable. Barna reported in a 2021 study of 25,000 teens from ages 13–17 and 26 countries, one-third believed in the resurrection of Jesus, and 50 percent of teens who identified as Christians believe in the resurrection of Jesus.[85] Combine these stats with the various studies mentioned in previous chapters, and it is obvious we are living in the ruins of a failed Christianity. Perhaps those words are jarring? Wright writes in his book, "The Resurrection of Jesus is the foundation of the Christian faith. To preach Christianity meant (to the Apostles) primarily to preach the Resurrection... The Resurrection is the central theme in every Christian sermon reported in Acts."[86] Every disciple who witnessed the risen Jesus died not for what they believed, but for what they saw. If the resurrection were just part of a conspiracy thought up by His followers, surely they would have recanted when they faced death?

The good news is even if we have failed, God has not. His Holy Spirit remains active in beckoning "all those who are weary and heavy laden to come to Him."[87] The same Barna study re-

---

84. Ibid

85. Barna. "Teens and Jesus." Barna Group, accessed July 1, 2023, https://www.barna.com/research/teens-and-jesus/.

86. N.T. Wright, *The Resurrection of the Son of God* (Minneapolis: Fortress Press, 2003), 3.

87. Matthew 11:28–30 (NIV)

vealed even those teens who did not identify as Christian have a positive view of Jesus. About half of all teens across faith groups describe Jesus as "loving" (49%) and believe he offers hope (46%) and cares about people (43%).[88] The global impression of Jesus is that he is trustworthy, generous, wise, peaceful… and the glowing list goes on.[89]

To create these deep wells, people who are seeking to mentor a disciple of the next generation need to focus on fostering a loving and inclusive community that values diversity and recognizes the image of God in every person. This means actively seeking out people who are different from us and getting to know them on a personal level. It means listening and learning from people who have different experiences and perspectives and striving to understand their stories and their struggles. It is worth noting that the meaning of words is constantly in flux depending on context and culture. It is for this reason I would caution anyone from reading the equivalent of the current political environment of diversity, equity, and inclusion, which is equated with a number of extremely controversial views and ideologies.

Discipleship in this context involves helping people deepen their understanding of God's love and grace and equipping them to live out these values in practical ways. What are those values? In Galatians 5:22–23, Paul lists nine specific behaviors: "love, joy, peace, forbearance, kindness, goodness, faithfulness, gentleness, and self-control."[90] It entails providing space for people to wrestle with theological questions and explore Scripture together in community. We must be willing to balance our own theological

88. "Barna. "Teens and Jesus." Barna Group, accessed July 1, 2023, https://www.barna.com/research/teens-and-jesus/."
89. "The Open Generation: A Global Teens Study." Tableau visualization, accessed April 16, 2023, https://public.tableau.com/views/TheOpenGenerationAGlobalTeensStudy/IntroCommunityIdentity-WorldandFaith?:language=en-US&:embed=y&:embed_code_version=3&:loadOrderID=0&:display_count=y&:origin=viz_share_link.
90. Galatians 5:22–23 (NIV)

traditions and spirit with the need to be open and inclusive to those who see things differently from us. Some suggest we must re-imagine the church as a missional movement. In the book The Starfish and the Spirit, Alan Hirsh states, "The Spirit is prodding his people to awaken to mission in their everyday life.[91]" He continues, "When the church is in mission, it is the true church. The church itself is not only a product of that mission but is obligated and destined to extend it by whatever means possible."[92] The mission of God flows directly through every believer and every community of faith that adheres to Jesus. To obstruct this is to block God's purposes in and through his people." If we must reimagine the church, it is only because we have gotten off mission. Our imaginations have strayed from God's original design.

The church growth movement of the late 1950s reimagined the church as a destination. As such, we began to program our worship and segment it. Modern-day churches have created "worship centers" at the "church." We've designed signs that we place at the entrance of these worship centers that say such things as "enter to worship" and "exit to serve." We've separated professional clergy and "reimagined" laity as a noun to include everyone else. Neither the words *clergy* nor *laity* appear in the Bible. While the body of Christ may have different gifts and callings, Paul refers to himself as brother and fellow servant (Colossians 4:7). We are all "servants of the Lord" (Romans 14:4). God never intended church to be a destination. Jesus did not go to the temple and set up shop while sending the disciples out to bring the people to Him. Jesus' ministry took place among the people. Church is not a place; church is an identity. Church is the embodiment of what it means to be Christ-like. First Peter 1:16 tells us to "be Holy for I am Holy."[93] Holiness is not a character trait of God;

---

91. Ford, Lance; Wegner, Rob; Hirsch, Alan. *The Starfish and the Spirit* (Exponential Series), 209. Kindle Edition. Zondervan.

92. Alan Hirsch. *The Forgotten Ways: Reactivating Apostolic Movements* (Grand Rapids: Brazos, 2016), 82.

93. 1 Peter 1:16 (NIV)

it is who God is and, therefore, who His church should be. Jesus' life was an invitation to relationship and, therefore, our lives should be lived invitational as well. Church is the people of God.

Ultimately, the goal of creating these deep wells is to help people stay centered on Jesus and everything that includes. Simultaneously, we resist the urge to be gatekeepers of our churches and faith with a litmus test for ideological agreement prior to being welcomed. Even in the midst of a divisive and polarized world, it is possible to dig these wells and invite others to drink *living water* from them. It is only at this point that we can begin to build a more unified and loving body of Christ that reflects God's heart for all people. Remember Agnes' story from chapter 3? Harry told Campolo he did not believe that a church that "throws birthday parties for 'prostitutes' at 3:30 in the morning exists, because if it did, I would join it."[94]

Little doubt, Harry had experienced the church as well-intentioned gatekeepers blocking access to the living water in deep wells. The Harries of this world often do not even know they need living water, much less desire it. But once they've experienced living water, chances are they will not wander far from it. I am concerned that when we Christians reimagined church, we imagined it more as a religious empire/institution than a movement of God and, in so doing, have developed amnesia and forgotten who we are. Empires and institutions build walls to protect their cities and their wealth. They build armies for self-defense. Institutions have machinery that perpetuates the institution. Institutions tend to focus on the survival of the institution. They tend to resist risk and play it safe. Dr. David Busic, one of five general superintendents for the Church of the Nazarene, stated, "God has not sent us to safe places to do easy things."[95] If the church is an institution and,

---

94. Tony Campolo, *The Kingdom of God Is a Party*.
95. David Busic, General Superintendent Church of the Nazarene, speech at General Assembly Church of the Nazarene, Indianapolis, IN, June 10, 2023.

as Christians, are simply punching a clock, checking off a list of responsibilities to get the job done, we'll never be fully committed to fulfilling the great commission. We will continue with a divided heart, and we will lose more and more subsequent generations. Make no mistake; the enemy is all in and fully committed to its mission to take as many to hell as possible.

Genesis 26 tells a story about Isaac, Abraham's Son. After the death of Abraham and during a time of famine, Isaac had settled in the valley of Gerar. Genesis 26:14 tells God had blessed Isaac, just like he had blessed Abraham, with "flocks and herds and a great household." Obviously, water was a primary need for Isaac, who was tasked with caring for so many people, but the Philistines had filled all the wells in with dirt. As a result, Isaac had to re-dig all the water wells his father had previously installed."[96] This required clearing the ground and removing the debris in order for the water to flow freely.

I'm concerned that sometimes we as the church have become so preoccupied with perpetuating the institution of the church that instead of pointing people towards the living water, we have become the debris blocking the water and even unintentionally filling the wells with dirt. We do this when we become entrenched in the politics of the empire or focus so much on popular cultural debates and the talking points of our favorite twenty-four-hour news source that we do not have time to spread the good news.

We often complain that the culture is increasingly hostile to Christianity. However, since the "moral majority" of the late '70s, Falwell declared "holy war."[97] Why are we surprised that they finally began to fight back? Our neighbors tend to be much more likely to know where we stand politically than they are where we stand spiritually. "People don't care how much you know until they

---

96. Genesis 26:18 (The Voice)
97. Doug Banwart, *Jerry Falwell, the Rise of the Moral Majority, and the 1980 Election*, Western Illinois Historical Review, vol. V, Spring 2013, ISSN 2153-1714.

know how much you care," is attributed to Theodore Roosevelt.[98] If we want the opportunity to point others to deep wells of living water, they must first know that we care. Judgment outside the context of a relationship is seldom effective. In other words, it does not seem consistent biblically or theologically to demand or expect anyone who does not claim a Christian identity to "lay down your life"[99] or even "love your neighbor as himself."[100]

Jesus Is The Way

"Jesus said to him, "I am the way and the truth and the life. No one comes to the Father except through me."[101]

In *The Mandalorian*, "the way" refers to the Mandalorian code: a code of conduct and a way of life followed by the Mandalorian warriors. This code emphasizes values such as honor, loyalty, and self-sufficiency. The Mandalorians prioritize survival, protecting their own, and adhering to their customs and traditions. Their way of life is centered around practical matters of survival and self-defense. The Mandalorians frequently espouse the phrase, "This is the way," during important moments as a reminder to each other that the Mandalorian code is not just a behavior; it is the core of their identity. Others will know them by their "way."

In the New Testament, Jesus often refers to Himself as "the way," expressing His role as the path to salvation, truth, and abundant life. Jesus proclaims, "I am the way and the truth and the life. No one comes to the Father except through me."[102] This statement serves as the cornerstone of Christian theology,

---

98. "People don't care how much you know until they know how much you care," Theodore Roosevelt, accessed June 16, 2023, https://www. thorpehouse.co.uk/headmasters-blog/2021/"no-one-cares-how-much-you-know-until-they-know-how-much-you-care"---president
99. John 15:13 (NIV)
100. John 15:13 (NIV)
101. John 14:6 (NRSV)
102. John 14:6 (NIV)

emphasizing that genuine connection with God and eternal life can only be found by following Jesus' teachings and example.

Just as the Mandalorians identified themselves as followers of "the way," Jesus' disciples frequently referred to themselves as followers of "the way." Jesus said of his disciples, "By this everyone will know that you are my disciples, if you love one another."[103] By contrast, historically, the term "Christian" was initially used as a form of derogatory labeling or even a slur. Its early usage was often associated with mockery, ridicule, and a negative connotation.[104] The origins of this can be traced back to the time when the term first emerged in the city of Antioch, as mentioned in the New Testament.

During the early days of the Christian movement, the followers of Jesus were a relatively small and distinct group within the diverse cultural and religious landscape of the Roman Empire. The term "Christianos" was coined by those outside the faith to distinguish this new religious sect from other groups, including Judaism, which was already recognized and protected under Roman law.[105]

The derogatory nature of the term likely stemmed from various factors. First, the Christians' belief in Jesus as the Messiah and their proclamation of His crucifixion and resurrection challenged the religious norms and authorities of the time. This led to suspicion, misunderstanding, and hostility from some members of the surrounding society.

Furthermore, the early Christians' refusal to worship the Roman gods and participate in the emperor cult was seen as an

---

103. John 13:35 (NIV)
104. Gwynn, David M., ed. The Oxford Encyclopedia of Early Christian Studies. Volume X. Oxford: Oxford University Press, 2019, s.v. "Christian," 123-125.
105. Certainly! Here's an example of a Chicago style footnote reference for the article "The Separation of Christianity from Judaism" written by Rebecca Denova and published on June 21, 2021, from World History Encyclopedia.

act of defiance against the established religious and political order. This defiance often attracted persecution and accusations of disloyalty or even atheism, further contributing to the negative perception of Christians.

As a result, the term Christian was initially used to mock and belittle the followers of Jesus, associating them with radicalism, superstition, or even criminal behavior. The Apostle Peter acknowledges this in his letter, stating, "If you suffer as a Christian, do not be ashamed, but praise God that you bear that name."[106]

However, over time, as the Christian movement grew and spread throughout the Roman Empire, the term Christian was reclaimed by the followers of Jesus. They embraced it as a mark of honor and identification with their faith, recognizing that suffering and persecution were part of their shared experience as disciples of Christ.[107]

Engaging Our Communities

One common question that arises within the Christian community is how to reconcile living out "the way" of Jesus in a world that, at best, remains unaware of His teachings and, in many cases, grows increasingly hostile towards them. This tension often poses a challenge for our churches, communities, and even within the broader culture.

As followers of Jesus, we are called to embrace His teachings and embody His way of life. Yet, it is undeniable that the values and principles of the world around us often diverge from those of Jesus. We find ourselves navigating a landscape where ignorance or even hostility towards the ways of Jesus can be prevalent.

In many countries, and even within certain pockets of the United States, the culture seems to be drifting further away from

---

106. 1 Peter 4:16 (NIV)
107. Rebecca Denova, "The Separation of Christianity from Judaism," World History Encyclopedia, accessed June 27, 2023, https://www.world-history.org/article/1785/the-separation-of-christianity-from-judaism.

the teachings of Jesus. The clash between the values of our faith and the prevailing cultural norms can create friction and challenge us to find a way to engage meaningfully without compromising our beliefs.

So, how do we reconcile "the way" of Jesus within such a complex context?

1. **Deepening our Faith:** It starts with a commitment to deepen our understanding of Jesus' teachings and His example. By immersing ourselves in His life, ministry, and the wisdom of the Scriptures, we can anchor ourselves in His truth and allow it to guide our decisions and actions. We must truly root our identity in Christ. Too often, we slap our Christian identity on top of other identities, such as our national identity, racial identity, or even gender identity, like a band-aid. One is not a male Christian, black or Jewish Christian. Nor should one claim they are a gay or heterosexual/cisgender Christian. Living in the way of Jesus and rooting our identity in Christ means Jesus is not an afterthought in our decisions but is primary in the choices we make. The Christian identity cannot be hyphenated.

2. **Theological humility:** The concept of theological humility reminds us that, regardless of our experience as Christians, our intelligence, our confidence, or our good works, we cannot claim to have an infallible interpretation of Scripture. Martin Luther's grievances with the Catholic Church, which eventually led to the Protestant Reformation, stemmed from the fact that the common people were entirely reliant on church officials for the reading and interpretation of Scripture. Since the Bible was written in Latin and the people spoke German, even if they could read, they would not have been able to understand it. This dependence on the church's interpretation allowed for abuses of authority, prompting Luther

to post his "95 Theses" on the door of the Castle Church in Wittenberg, Germany.[108]

Today, we recognize the flaws in such practices and thinking and the inherent dangers of concentrated power in the hands of a few. It often leads to abuse and persecution. We must learn from past mistakes and be self-aware enough to acknowledge the fragility of human understanding, especially when dealing with a text that is over 2000 years old and rooted in an ancient culture. Our interpretations of Scripture are inevitably influenced by our own experiences.

When it comes to interpreting Scripture and defining Christian practices, it is wise to rely on the traditions of the early church and their interpretations. The creeds, which have stood the test of time, can serve as a reliable measure of the essential aspects of the Christian faith. By drawing upon these established foundations, we can navigate the complexities of biblical interpretation with humility and a greater understanding of our shared Christian identity.

3. **Authentic Discipleship:** We are called to be authentic disciples of Jesus, not only in our personal lives but also as a community. This means embracing His teachings and embodying His love, grace, and compassion in our interactions with others. Our lives should reflect the transformative power of following Jesus.

4. **Authentic Relationships:** In ancient Jewish culture, the Talmid/Rabbi connection was a deep relationship. I will expand further on the Talmid/Rabbi relationship in chapter five, but for now, it suffices to say that it is the same model Jesus used with his disciples, and thus, it is the model they followed after Jesus' death to continue the movement Jesus started. Immediately after Pentecost,

---

108. Dixon, C Scott, *Martin Luther and the Reformation in Historical Thought, 1517–2017. Studies: An Irish Quarterly Review* 106, no. 424 (2017): 404–16. https://www.jstor.org/stable/90015885.

Peter and the others fanned across the Roman Empire and continued where Jesus left off. They loved the unlovable, touched the untouchable, and they heard the voiceless, and they saw the invisible. If the church wants to repair its relationship with its communities, perhaps that is where it should begin.

The Japanese art of mending things with gold is commonly known as "Kintsugi." Kintsugi, which translates to "golden joinery" or "golden repair," is a traditional Japanese technique that involves repairing broken pottery or ceramics by filling the cracks with lacquer mixed with gold, silver, or other precious metals.[109] This method emphasizes the beauty of the imperfections and the history of the object, turning the damage into a part of its story. Kintsugi is seen as a metaphor for embracing flaws and finding beauty in the process of healing and restoration. It treats breakage repair as part of the history of an object rather than something to disguise. It is a philosophy that embraces the flaws and imperfection, and in doing so, we make something much stronger and more beautiful. Perhaps you also see the parallels to ministry in this philosophy, as do I.

5. **Engaging the Culture:** Rather than retreating or withdrawing from the culture, we are called to engage with it. This engagement should be marked by respect, understanding, and a genuine desire to build bridges. By engaging thoughtfully, we can demonstrate the relevance and beauty of Jesus' teachings, even in the face of hostility or ignorance.

6. **Prayer and Dependence on God:** Recognizing our limitations, we must fervently seek God's guidance and rely on His strength. Through prayer, we can find wisdom,

---

109. "Kintsugi: The Japanese Art of Golden Repair," Traditional Kyoto, accessed July 1, 2023, https://traditionalkyoto.com/culture/kintsugi/.

discernment, and the courage to navigate the tensions and challenges that arise as we live out "the way" of Jesus.

7. **Recover Childlike Wonder**: In his book *The Life You've Always Wanted*, John Ortberg recounts a story from when his children were small. He had a custom of bathing his children together to save time. Of course, he knew the ritual would eventually have to end. He recalls that his son Johnny was still in the tub, and Laura was out safely in her pajamas. He says:

I was attempting to dry off Mallory, who had already left the water. However, she started doing what our family refers to as the Dee Dah Day dance. This involved her running around in circles and repeatedly singing, "Dee dah day, dee day, day." The dance was a simple yet expressive way for her to convey immense joy. When her happiness overflowed and words were insufficient to express her euphoria, she resorted to dancing. And so, she performed the Dee Dah Day dance.

At that moment, I was feeling irritated and urged Mallory to hurry. In response, she intensified her circling and chanted "dee dah day" even faster. "No, Mallory, that's not what I meant! Stop with the Dee Dah Day routine and come here so I can dry you off. Hurry!"

Then she posed a profound question: "Why?"

I couldn't provide an answer. I had nowhere to be, nothing urgent to do, no appointments or sermons to write. I had become so accustomed to rushing, so consumed by my own narrow agenda, and trapped in the monotonous cycle of moving from one task to the next. Meanwhile, here was life, here was joy, and right in front of me was an invitation to dance—an invitation I was overlooking.[110]

---

110. Ortberg, John. "Living Life as a Series of Dee Dah Day Moments." MarriageTrac, accessed July 1, 2023. https://www.marriagetrac.com/living-life-as-a-series-of-dee-dah-day-moments/.

Sometimes, after we've been serving God for a while, we can fall into a trap of busyness and lose our childlike wonderment (joy). Be intentionally curious. Be willing to ask why. Just because the church has always done it a certain way does not mean we always have to do it the same way. Our message can remain consistent, and we can try new ways. Curiosity stokes joy. It reminds us not to get so busy working for the kingdom that we forget to worship him and keep our faith fresh. The decision to follow Jesus is not a solitary decision made in a single moment. It is a decision we make every day when we wake up and often multiple times a day. Each time, we give God permission to "do it again."

While the tension between "the way" of Jesus and the prevailing culture may persist, we can find solace and encouragement in knowing that throughout history, the followers of Jesus have faced similar challenges. By remaining steadfast in our faith, being a beacon of love and truth, and trusting in God's faithfulness, we can navigate this tension and make a positive impact on the world around us.

Within the rich tapestry of Christianity, we find diverse expressions of faith and theological frameworks that shape our understanding of what it means to be a follower of Christ. Two concepts that hold profound significance in this journey are the early Christian label as "followers of the way" and the modern theological framework of "centered set." Here, we will explore the similarities and differences between these two approaches, highlighting the importance of living a lifestyle reflective of a Christ follower.

The Early Christians as "Followers of The Way"

The term "followers of the Way" used to describe those who dedicated themselves to Jesus, highlights their deep commitment to living according to Jesus' teachings and example (Acts 9:2). The label followers of the way indicated their commitment to following the teachings and example of Jesus Christ. The label of "Way" emphasized the centrality of Jesus as the way, the truth, and the life (John 14:6) and highlighted the importance of living in accordance with His teachings.

Centered Set Theology and Proximity to Christ

Centered set theology, on the other hand, focuses on the concept of proximity to Christ as the defining characteristic of a Christ-centered life.[111] It recognizes that the Christian journey is not merely about adherence to a set of beliefs or static boundaries but rather about dynamically moving closer to Jesus and continually aligning oneself with His teachings and example.

In a centered set approach, individuals are seen as moving toward or away from Christ, with their proximity to Him determining their spiritual orientation. The focus is on cultivating a vibrant, transformative relationship with Jesus and allowing His presence and influence to shape every aspect of life. In other words, unlike bounded set theology, which focuses on who is in and who is out based upon how well someone acquiesces to the rules, which upon close examination are often more contextual than biblical, centered set is proximity. Proximity matters. If you want to be warm, get near the fire. It is the source of warmth. Jesus told the woman at the well he was the source of living water.[112] If people want living water, they must have access to the source.

Similarities and Synergies

While the early Christian label as "followers of the way" and centered set theology may differ in terminology and historical context, they share fundamental similarities and can mutually enrich our understanding of Christian discipleship.

Relational Focus: Both concepts prioritize the significance of relationship and proximity to Jesus. The early Christians sought to emulate Jesus' teachings and way of life, while centered set theology emphasizes the dynamic journey of drawing closer to Christ.

---

111. https://shalomcarcoar.com/2017/02/12/digging-wells-or-building-fences/

112. John 4:13–14 (NIV)

Directional Movement: Both frameworks recognize the importance of intentional movement and growth. Early Christians were called to continuously walk in the footsteps of Jesus, while centered set theology invites believers to actively progress toward Christ and align their lives with His teachings.

Reflective Lifestyle: Both concepts call for a lifestyle that reflects the values, ethics, and character of Jesus. Whether it is following "the way" or moving within a centered set, the focus is on embodying a Christ-like life that demonstrates love, grace, justice, and compassion.

End of Chapter 4 Summary: Leading by Example

The early Christian label as "followers of the way" and centered set theology offer complementary perspectives on what it means to live as a Christ follower. While one is rooted in the historical context of the early church, and the other is a contemporary theological framework, both highlight the importance of living a lifestyle reflective of a Christ-centered life. That is to say, if we want to mentor the next generations, we must lead by example.

As we embrace our identity as followers of the way, let us also recognize the dynamic journey of drawing closer to Christ and aligning ourselves with His teachings in a centered set framework. By pursuing an authentic and transformative relationship with Jesus, we can walk in the footsteps of the early Christians, lead by example, and strive to reflect His love and truth in all aspects of our lives.

Principles for Building Bridges to Culture and Community with Your Transformative Identity

Principle 1: Rooted and Relational Faith
Start by deepening your faith in Jesus and rooting your identity in Him. This means immersing yourself in His teachings, His life, and the wisdom of the Scriptures. Understand that your Christian identity should not be hyphenated; it is primary in your decision-making. Embrace theological humility, recognizing that

human understanding is fallible, and rely on the traditions of the early church to navigate biblical interpretation. Your faith is both deeply rooted and open to growth, mirroring the concept of a centered set theology that focuses on proximity to Christ.

Principle 2: Authentic Discipleship and Relationships

Embrace authentic discipleship in your personal life and as a community. This entails embodying Jesus' love, grace, and compassion in your interactions with others. Be like the early followers of Jesus who loved the unlovable, touched the untouchable, heard the voiceless, and saw the invisible. Foster authentic relationships by following the Talmid/Rabbi model, deepening connections within your community, and repairing broken relationships with a spirit of grace, as exemplified by the Japanese art of Kintsugi. This authenticity and restoration mirror the transformative power of following Jesus.

Principle 3: Engagement and Childlike Wonder

Engage with the culture around you rather than retreating from it. Approach this engagement with respect, understanding, and a genuine desire to build bridges. Demonstrate the relevance and beauty of Jesus' teachings even in the face of hostility or ignorance. Maintain a posture of curiosity and childlike wonder, asking "why" and being open to new ways of expressing your faith. Avoid falling into the trap of busyness and maintain your sense of joy and wonder, recognizing that the decision to follow Jesus is a daily one, not a rigid set of rules.

A Prayer for Leading by Example and Building Bridges to Others Through Our Transformative Identity

Dear Lord,

Guide us to be true followers of Your way, not merely a way. Grant us the wisdom to preach through our actions, reserving words for when they are truly needed. Restore within us the childlike wonder that fuels curiosity, for it is through curiosity that we continue to learn and grow.

Instill in our hearts a deep sense of gratitude, helping us avoid the relentless trap of busyness that can distract us from Your presence. May we walk the path where Jesus walked, mirroring the love and compassion of the early disciples who embraced the unlovable, reached out to the untouchable, listened to the voiceless, and saw the invisible among us.

Above all, Lord, anchor our faith in You, not in the confines of institutional boundaries. Ignite in us a profound love for Your church, that our lives may shine as a testament to our love for one another.

In Your holy name, we pray.

Amen.

Reachable Questions for Reflection

1. After reading this chapter, what are your thoughts about the new creation?
2. What is your understanding of deep wells?
3. Do you agree with the author that one key to revitalizing our churches and fulfilling our purpose as followers of Jesus is to be sure we are not creating obstacles to living water? (Why or why not?)
4. Considering the current divisions that are so prevalent in society today, how do we reconcile "the way" of Jesus with a holy life?
5. Discuss the art of Kintsugi and how you think it relates to discipleship.

Chapter 5

Dancing with the Divine
Embracing Christ's Example for Life Transformation

"Then Jesus said to his disciples, 'Whoever wants to be my disciple must deny themselves and take up their cross and follow me.'" [113]

Relationships Are the Oil of Faith

"Can the church stop its puny, hack dreams of trying to 'make a difference in the world' and start dreaming God-sized dreams of making the world different?"[114]—Leonard Sweet.

Our modern world yearns for a meaningful connection with the divine, but not with just any god. What our world truly craves is a profound relationship with a God of depth and authenticity, a God embodying integrity and overflowing grace. The time of harmful religious practices, where individuals sought to pacify an angered deity through rigidly prescribed rituals, is now a thing of the past. Instead, the search is on for a God who breathes life into existence. [115] As we wring our hands in despair for the next generation and beyond, we pray, "Dear Jesus, we have a problem in your church today." Jesus writes back, "Dear church, read the letters. Understand who you are, understand what I created you

---

113. Matthew 16:24 (NIV)
114. Sweet, Leonard. *Soul Tsunami*. Zondervan, 1999.
115. Gunter II, Dwight M.. *Seven Letters to Seven Churches: Lessons from the Book of Revelation*. Beacon Hill Press of Kansas City, Kindle Edition.

to be, understand why I have freed you and what I have formed you to be. Then do what you're supposed to do."[116]

The Allure of the Ultimate Solution: The Magic Formula Pursuit

Throughout history, humanity's search for a panacea—whether called the "knowledge of good and evil," power, or eternal life—echoes the yearning for an elusive formula that promises fulfillment. From Adam and Eve's pursuit of divine knowledge to Ponce de Leon's quest for the Fountain of Youth, these aspirations reflect the timeless quest for answers. Often, the church has looked to models from corporate America to other religious traditions while failing to recognize one of the first answers we learned in Sunday school, assuming we attended church as a child. *Jesus is always the answer.*

Climbing Trees in Search of the Messiah

Perhaps the familiar story, for some, of Zacchaeus can give us an example of such desperation that one would go to extraordinary lengths to come and receive. Luke 14 tells us that Zacchaeus was "short in stature."[117] It also tells us that He was a "chief tax collector and was wealthy." In other words, he was not only a thief, but he was also a thief who stole from his own people. He not only stole from his own people, but he was also a stooge of the very empire that was occupying Jerusalem, the land God had promised and ultimately gifted to the descendants of Abraham. He was loathed. Despite all his wealth and power, Zacchaeus still came up short, not just in stature but in life. He had spent his life following the rules of the empire to climb higher within its structures, only to abandon the Lord and His ways. Zacchaeus had to climb a tree just to catch a glimpse of Jesus. He partnered with the empire, thinking it would guarantee safety and security, but in the end, he was alone, unsafe, and insecure, craning his

---

116. Ibid
117. Luke 19 (NIV)

neck just to catch a glimpse of the man about whom everyone was seemingly talking. Was this the long-awaited Messiah? If it was, Zacchaeus would surely not be counted among those who would be offered salvation. Hence, the tree serves a dual purpose for Zacchaeus. Ashamed of his choices, the tree also provides a hiding place for him.

As loathed and ashamed as Zacchaeus was, though, he was not the first to hide. Adam and Eve once had everything. Genesis tells us they received a daily invitation to walk with God in the cool of the day within paradise.[118] Unfortunately, they believed the adversary's lie that God was reneging on His promises and provision to them, and so they disobeyed God's only rule. Do not eat of the fruit of the tree of the knowledge of Good and evil.[119] The next time they receive an invitation to dance with the divine, they hide. Fortunately, that is not the end of the story. Instead of leaving them to die, the original promised consequence of eating the forbidden fruit, God calls them out of hiding.[120]

Called out of Hiding

I'm reminded of a story found in an old but popular book, *All I Ever Needed to Know I Learned in Kindergarten* by Robert Fulghum.

> In the early dry dark of an October's Saturday evening, the neighborhood children are playing hide-and-seek. How long since I played hide-and-seek? Thirty years, maybe more. I remember how. I could become part of the game in a moment, if invited. Adults don't play hide-and-seek. Not for fun, anyway. Too bad.
>
> Did you have a kid in your neighborhood who always hid so good, nobody could find him? We did. After a while, we would give up on him and go off, leaving him to rot wherever he was. Sooner or later, he would show up, all mad because we didn't keep looking for him. And we would get mad back

---

118. Genesis 1:16–17 (NRSV)
119. Genesis 3:1–6 (NRSV)
120. Genesis 3:8 (NRSV)

because he wasn't playing the game the way it was supposed to be played. There's hiding and there's finding, we'd say. And he'd say it was hide-and-seek, not hide-and-give-UP, and we'd all yell about who made the rules and who cared about who, anyway, and how we wouldn't play with him anymore if he didn't get it straight and who needed him anyhow, and things like that. Hide-and-seek-and-yell. No matter what, though, the next time, he would hide too good again. He's probably still hidden somewhere, for all I know.

As I write this, the neighborhood game goes on, and there is a kid under a pile of leaves in the yard just under my window. He has been there a long time now, and everybody else is found and they are about to give up on him over at the base. I considered going out to the base and telling them where he is hiding. And I thought about setting the leaves on fire to drive him out. Finally, I just yelled, "GET FOUND, KID!" out the window. And scared him so bad he probably wet his pants and started crying and ran home to tell his mother. It's really hard to know how to be helpful sometimes.

A man I know found out last year he had terminal cancer. He was a doctor. And knew about dying, and he didn't want to make his family and friends suffer through that with him. So he kept his secret. And died. Everybody said how brave he was to bear his suffering in silence and not tell everybody, and so on and so forth. But privately, his family and friends said how angry they were that he didn't need them, didn't trust their strength. And it hurt that he didn't say goodbye.

He hid too well. Getting found would have kept him in the game. Hide-and-seek, grown-up style. Wanting to hide. Needing to be sought. Confused about being found. "I don't want anyone to know." "What will people think?" "I don't want to bother anyone."

Better than hide-and-seek, I like the game called Sardines. In Sardines, the person who is It goes and hides, and everybody goes looking for him. When you find him, you get in with him and hide there with him. Pretty soon, everybody is hiding together, all stacked in a small space like puppies in a pile. And pretty soon, somebody giggles, and somebody laughs, and everybody gets found.

Medieval theologians even described God in hide-and-seek terms, calling him *Deus Absconditus*. But me, I think old God is a Sardine player. And will be found the same way everybody gets found in Sardines—by the sound of laughter of those heaped together at the end.

"Olly-olly-oxen-free." The kids out in the street are hollering the cry that says, "Come on in, wherever you are. It's a new game." And so say I. To all those who have hid too good. *Get found, kid!* Olly-olly-oxen-free.

The irony of sin is it promises to give us the desires of our heart but deprives us of the thing we need most: connection with our creator and each other. Just as it drove Adam and Eve to hide in the bushes from God when he came, it drove Zacchaeus to hide in the tree when Jesus came, and it continues to drive us into hiding today. The result is a deep, dark void that many recognize exists but struggle to identify the source of their pain or struggle. As a result, they seek to fill the void with things like fame, fortune, and even family. The adversary continues to deceive, offering just enough hope to keep people trapped in the game of sin but not enough hope to allow them to turn away from the vice of sin and unto Jesus.

I'm reminded of a scene from the blockbuster movie *The Hunger Games*, which was based on the popular novel series. In *Mockingjay Part 1*, President Snow is talking to the designer of the Hunger Games, and he tells him, "Hope is the only thing stronger than fear. A little hope is effective. A lot of hope is dangerous.[121]"

That is exactly the game the adversary tries to play in our lives. The aftermath of this grand deception has woven a curious tapestry. Within its threads, people find themselves clinging desperately to slivers of hope. They reach for the forbidden fruit promised by all of the false Messiahs of the world, the glittering

---

121. *The Hunger Games*. Directed by Gary Ross. Lionsgate, 2012.

allure of fame and fortune, and the eerie embrace of cultic leaders who vilify the world outside their fold. All these fragments serve as beacons in a fog of uncertainty, severing connections to those who genuinely care and even casting shadows upon families.

Yet, there lies another layer to this tale. Among the disillusioned, those who've tasted the forbidden fruit's bitter taste of false hope, a different path emerges. Frustration pushes them to abandon that elusive light, and they dive into the depths of outer darkness. They hide from their pain and seek solace in the pixelated realms of pornography, in the synthetic highs offered by drugs, and in the numbing haze of alcohol. These become their hiding places from a reality that feels like a cruel prank. The grand deception's aftermath isn't just a story of clinging and yearning, but also one of evasive retreats and the search for an alternate, albeit fleeting, existence. There are millions in hiding. They've lost hope and are on the verge of despair if they aren't there already. To them, we extend an invitation: "Olly, olly oxen free!" It's time to come home. Get found!

No matter how glorious a nation may seem, no rendition of an empire, no matter how sterling a politician, and not even the most impeccable family unit can evade the inevitable letdown of a life void of Jesus. They stumble and falter, unable to mend the chasm that yawns within, for what's absent isn't a mere puzzle piece; it's an identity. A piece of the soul can only be rekindled through an intimate connection with the architect of the universe, the creator of the cosmos, Jesus Christ—God incarnate. The true salve for that aching void is an identity unearthed in the profound embrace of this cosmic architect, fostering a bond that transcends all the fleeting glamour this world has to offer.

Indeed, what Adam and Eve forfeited, Zacchaeus yearned to perceive from a treetop view. This essence is what the succeeding generation ardently seeks to grasp, yet they lack mentors to introduce them to it. They are desperately wanting to be found but are afraid to hope again. The emptiness resonates, a sense that something vital is absent. Desperation for connection drives some to discard their human identity entirely. They adopt new identities as animals, like cats or dogs, as they grasp for belonging. It's as if, having been discarded and exploited by society, they choose to forfeit the true identity that's been hidden and masked from them.

Their yearning echoes the very desire that has led countless to stretch their necks to catch a glimpse of the manifestation of God in human form. This longing is to witness grace incarnate, a living, breathing embodiment of divine love woven into human lives. These actions could be seen as akin to Zacchaeus ascending the Sycamore tree, craving a mere glimpse of God in the flesh—a yearning that transcends time.[122]

Some people often venture into uncharted realms, far beyond the boundaries of their wildest imaginations, as humanity hungers for an encounter that defies conventions. What fuels this insatiable yearning? None other than the fervent desire to witness God in the fullness of life, pulsating with every breath—an authenticity that transcends mere theory. Their souls cry out, yearning for sustenance, craving the tangibility of a God who doesn't dwell in the realm of abstraction.

The hunger is undeniable, a relentless gnawing that pierces the core of their being. But here's the twist, my friend—we can't simply discourse about it. No, that won't suffice. This isn't a pursuit marked by wistful dreams alone. The call resounds with urgency: we must allow the Holy Spirit to infuse real life into our souls and become living testaments to this sacred reality.

Imagine this journey as a tapestry woven with threads of aspiration and intention. Yet, the tapestry remains incomplete unless each strand, each intention, and each desire is meticulously woven into the fabric of our existence. A symphony of actions is required, a harmonious dance that bridges the chasm between yearning and fulfillment.

---

122. Gunter II, Dwight M. *Seven Letters to Seven Churches: Lessons from the Book of Revelation.* Beacon Hill Press of Kansas City, Kindle Edition.

So, let the clarion call be heard: we are not mere spectators in this cosmic theater. We are the players, the conduits of this grand transformation. Our role is clear, the script etched within the very essence of our being. To sate this hunger, we must be the embodiment of the divine breath, the living manifestation of the God *they* seek. This isn't about casting hopeful glances; it's about becoming the living, breathing embodiment of hope itself.

In a world beset by wishful thinking and transient desires, the mandate is simple yet profound: we must be the living revelation, a testament to a God whose existence is undeniable. So, let us shatter the illusion of passive yearning and embrace the exhilarating journey of living out the divine narrative. Our lives, our actions, our very essence—these are the chapters that script the grand saga of a God that lives and breathes within us.

Embarking on the eternal odyssey of humanity's relentless pursuit of ultimate truths, the very essence of discipleship emerges as a north star guiding our way, akin to the fervor propelling scientific explorations. As we turn the pages of this chapter, we venture into the mystical interplay between this profound quest and the intricate dance of discipleship—a convergence where spiritual yearning and scientific curiosity intertwine in a cosmic waltz.

Embracing Responsibility
Unleashing the Strength of Accountability

In certain circles, "accountability" has sadly donned a negative cloak nowadays. However, within the realm of mentoring, particularly in the delicate art of nurturing a Christian identity, accountability stands as a radiant gem. It emerges as a potent elixir, orchestrating a symphony of transformational notes. Through its enchanting rhythm, people are gently guided towards weaving fresh threads of habit, each thread contributing to the tapestry of their most noble selves and aspirations. The investigators of accountability unearthed a fascinating spectrum of probabilities governing goal achievement through various stages of action:

- The inception of an idea or goal: A mere 10 percent likelihood of completion
- The conscious commitment to undertake the task: This escalates to a 25 percent probability
- Designating a specific time for its execution: This marks a leap to a 40 percent chance
- Crafting a meticulous plan outlining the hows: The odds rise to 50 percent
- Vowing to someone that you're bound to execute it: This vaults to a promising 65 percent
- Orchestrating a precise accountability rendezvous with your committed confidant: This skyrockets to an impressive 95 percent assurance[123]

Even Aristotle believed the best way to become better people is to submit to a master. Learn to ride a horse by finding a master/mentor and becoming an apprentice.[124] Perhaps this shaping, accountability, and mentoring might be seen as a grand choreographed dance.

The Divine Dance

One of my favorite depictions of the Trinity comes from the icon of Rublev. Stepping into the realm of the icon of Rublev, we see art and devotion intertwine to craft an extraordinary tale of spiritual depth and artistic brilliance. It's like stepping through a portal into a world where beauty and divinity dance hand in hand.

The icon is a canvas bathed in the glow of history, a canvas that Andrei Rublev himself breathed life into centuries ago. In this sacred scene, a trio of celestial figures gathers around a simple table,

123. "The Power of Accountability." The Standard, 2018, Volume 49, Issue 3. AFCPE. Accessed August 17, 2023. https://www.afcpe.org/news-and-publications/the-standard/2018-3/the-power-of-accountability/
124. "3 Great Mentoring Relationships Throughout History." Mentor Resources Blog. Mentor Resources, Accessed August 17, 2023. https://www.mentorresources.com/mentoring-blog/3-great-mentoring-relationships-throughout-history.

an intimate symposium of the divine. These angelic beings exude an otherworldly serenity, their gazes locked in a dance of mutual admiration, their gestures an intricate choreography of unity.

The color palette employed by Rublev is a masterpiece in and of itself. Deep blue is reminiscent of the expanse of the heavens enveloping the figures, while earthy tones and glistening gold infuse the scene with a touch of the earthly and the divine. Look closer, and you'll find intricate patterns adorning their robes—golden threads weaving a tapestry of cosmic wisdom and celestial geometry.

But this icon is no mere painting; it's an invitation—a whispered call to engage with the mystery of the Holy Trinity. As light dances upon the surface, it kindles the gentle expressions on the angelic faces, as if the very act of gazing upon it draws you into an eternal embrace that defies time and space.

The icon of Rublev isn't just pigment on wood; it's a window to the infinite, a passage to a truth that transcends cultures and eras. It's not just about the artistry; it's about the boundless love that ties Father, Son, and Holy Spirit in a cosmic dance, inviting us to join in this divine rhythm. The relationship embodied by the Godhead is a depiction of the relationship God desires for humanity with Himself, and it is the relationship intended between the Rabbi and his Talmud. Finally, it is that relationship we should seek to mirror with those we are discipling. A divine dance set to the tune of a love song written by the creator himself and lived out in the life of Jesus.

Much like the intrepid minds of history plumbing the depths of reality's enigma, the ancient disciples craved not only knowledge but this deeper connection, seeking their Rabbi's wisdom to illuminate the tangled paths of existence. Discipleship in "the way" of Jesus is closer to any panacea we could ever find on our own. Let us explore the way of the Rabbi as a model of how we disciple the next generation and beyond.

Learning from History:
Navigating the Path of Transformation

By transitioning to the present, the narrative turns to the task of engaging the next generation within the church. It scrutinizes their distinct approaches to faith, uncovering the influences that shape their spiritual identities and aspirations.

At the heart of connecting with the younger generation lies a potent act—an invitation. This chapter delves into the transformative force of inviting young individuals into authentic, loving relationships. Such connections bridge generations and foster an environment of empathy and acceptance.

Love's Transformative Role: The Keystone Ingredient

Amidst the intricate findings of my research, one truth resounds—the profound potency of love. Anchored in love, the pursuit of relevance and connection takes on new dimensions, influencing the church's role in the lives of Millennials annd Gen Z.

Rediscovering the Master's Blueprint:
The Timeless Wisdom of Discipleship

Revisiting the teachings of Jesus, let's delve into the essence of discipleship in its purest form. By analyzing Jesus' interactions with His disciples, it uncovers the core of true discipleship—intimate learning, close following, and mirroring the Master. As we learn to dance with the divine, they will also learn.

In a dramatic shift, conventional approaches to church growth and engagement are challenged. The call to transition from attraction-based strategies to active participation in the divine narrative takes center stage, emphasizing the transformative power of embodying Christ's example.

The Rabbi's Dust

Imagine stepping into the tapestry of discipleship, where words echo like ancient melodies, and the canvas is woven with threads of community and commitment. Discipleship—more than a mere churchy phrase, is a symphony of understanding that beckons questions: Do we truly grasp its essence? Do we comprehend its intricate layers that span time and tradition? Let us venture deeper into this mosaic.

Envision the vibrant "village life"—an insula pulsating with extended family bonds. Grandpas, grandmas, moms, dads, cousins, uncles, aunts—an interwoven web of hearts residing around a courtyard where laughter dances in harmony. Their lives are not solitary notes; they are a harmonious composition. Interdependence binds them as they share their occupation, their devotion to God, and a journey to Jerusalem's feasts—a collective pilgrimage on this road called life. Through life's peaks and valleys, they embrace one another, offering encouragement and gentle correction. This is more than mere living—it's discipleship's nucleus in a world that values the other over self. One hears the echoes of the Deuteronomic text the ancient Hebrew referred to as the shama (שָׁמַע). Shama in Hebrew is translated as hear, listen, or give attention. It begins in Deuteronomy 6:4–9: "Hear, O Israel: The Lord is our God, the Lord alone. You shall love the Lord your God with all your heart, and with all your soul, and with all your might. Keep these words that I am commanding you today in your heart. Recite them to your children and talk about them when you are at home and when you are away, when you lie down and when you rise. Bind them as a sign on your hand, fix them as an emblem on your forehead, and write them on the doorposts of your house and on your gates." It is also repeated in Deuteronomy 11:13–21 and Numbers 15:37–41.

Hear also the words of Jesus reverberate through Jerusalem as the religious elites spring their trap to ensnare Jesus in an attempt to prove Him to be a false prophet. But Jesus, recognizing their trap, turns the tables on them, and the plot fails. Another one of the teachers of the law inquires of Jesus, "which is the greatest commandment, to which Jesus recites the shama, but ties it to loving your neighbor as yourself.[125]

Now, set your gaze upon the illuminated scrolls, the Torah and Tanakh—the sacred words that transcend parchment. They are not mere ink and paper; they are the symphony of divine revelation, the heartbeat of an ancient connection. Picture the faithful dancing in jubilation, their lips brushing the scroll with reverence, a kiss of devotion. The synagogue hums with fervor as Rabbis or learned guests expound upon these scriptures. But knowledge isn't the end; it's a threshold.

Travel to the yesteryears when schools reverberated with the scribbles of future disciples. The Torah becomes their foundation; by twelve or thirteen, they can recite its verses with a wisdom beyond their years. Here, amidst the wisdom of ages, the distinction between boys and girls is blurred by a shared pursuit of enlightenment. Beyond these corridors, some journey further—enter the Beti (HA) Midrash, where passionate seekers transform into torchbearers of wisdom. It is within these walls and carefully designed environment that extraordinary individuals begin to take shape.

Finally, behold the Talmidim, the devoted disciples who step into the sacred dance with their Rabbis. These are the best of the best. If this were the Air Force, they'd be your top gun pilots. Unlike casual students, these disciples are not content with mimicking words. Their goal is transformation, becoming a living reflection of their teacher. This journey isn't undertaken lightly; it comes at a cost—a cost they willingly pay. In their pursuit, they aim to be covered in the dust of their Rabbi, sharing not just space but a profound connection. Imagine this level of intimacy—closer than breath in a world that champions distance.

Consider these verses, these fragments of truth: 2 Corinthians 3:18 speaks of transformation, a crescendo from glory to glory; 1 Corinthians 11:1 beckons us to be imitators, to reflect Christ's

125. Mark 12:29-31 (NRSV)

image; and Ephesians 4:15 calls for growth, for us to become one with the head, Christ. This is discipleship—a rhythm that transcends time.

In this symphony, the question resounds: Are we Talmidim, true disciples? Do we inhale and exhale the essence of Christ? Is our heartbeat synchronized with His purpose? From dawn to dusk, do we echo the mission of Christ in every thought, every action? The great ones of history—Elijah, Elisha, Paul, and Timothy—answered this call, following their teachers with devotion. In this grand tapestry, we each find our role, our brushstroke, in the masterpiece of discipleship.

This is the model of discipleship to which God calls and Jesus embodied. In the sermon on the mount found in Matthew 5–7. This will become known as the greatest sermon ever preached. Jesus climbed the mountain and those who climbed with Him, are the ones who heard. "Hear, O people of God: Obey! The Lord is our God, the Lord alone. You shall love the Lord your God with all your heart, and with all your soul, and with all your might. Keep these words that I am commanding you today in your heart. Recite them to your children and talk about them when you are at home and when you are away, when you lie down, and when you rise. Bind them as a sign on your hand, fix them as an emblem on your forehead, and write them on the doorposts of your house and on your gates."

End of Chapter 5 Summary: Dancing with the Divine

In this chapter, the sacred journey of Christian discipleship is explored through the lens of the icon of Rublev, symbolizing the divine relationship within the Holy Trinity. This metaphor invites believers to engage in a dance with the divine, delving into the mysteries of faith. The model of discipleship proposed, inspired by Jesus, challenges conventional approaches by choosing disciples from unexpected backgrounds, emphasizing love as a transformative force. The call is to shift from attraction-based strategies to embody Christ's example, fostering a harmonious environment of interdependence and shared wisdom. Embracing the role of Talmidim, true disciples, and living out the Shema can powerfully transform the discipleship narrative for generations to come.

I am calling upon us to shift our focus away from attraction-based strategies, and instead, I urge us to emulate Christ's example and become living reflections of His mission. Discipleship is like a beautiful composition, where interdependence and shared wisdom come together to create a nurturing environment. Ultimately, I believe that our greatest success in reaching the next generations will come when our lives, intertwined in a divine dance, become the true attraction. When others witness the completeness of such a relationship, they will desire it for their own lives.

By living out the Shema—loving the Lord with all our hearts, souls, and might—and passing down this profound faith to the next generation, we can actively and powerfully transform the practice of discipleship.

Principles for Embracing Christ's Example for Life Transformation

Principle 1: Embrace the Divine Dance of Love

Like the icon of Rublev symbolizing the unity within the Holy Trinity, recognize that the essence of faith lies in a profound relationship with God. Embrace the divine dance of love by nurturing authentic, loving relationships within your faith community. Just as Father, Son, and Holy Spirit share an eternal bond, seek to bridge generations through empathy and acceptance, inviting others into this cosmic rhythm of love.

Principle 2: Become a Talmidim—A True Disciple

Discipleship is not a passive endeavor but an active and transformative journey. Follow the model of the Talmidim, the devoted disciples who sought to mirror their teacher, Jesus, in every aspect of their lives. Strive for intimacy with Christ, inhaling and exhaling His essence, and let His mission become your heartbeat. Be willing to pay the cost of becoming covered in the dust of your Rabbi, walking in His footsteps, and mirroring His image in your daily actions.

Principle 3: Pass Down the Faith

Just as the biblical command instructs, love the Lord with all your heart, soul, and might, and pass down this profound faith to the next generation. Recognize that discipleship is not limited to knowledge but includes sharing the wisdom and love of Christ with others. Create an environment where young individuals can connect with the sacred and experience the transformative power of love. Encourage intergenerational relationships within your faith community, ensuring that the faith is not only learned but lived out in a way that reflects the presence of God.

A Prayer for Dancing with the Divine and Embracing Christ's Example for Life Transformation

Lord, we express our gratitude, firstly for extending to us the invitation to dance with You and secondly, for being our guiding teacher in this divine dance. We thank You for Your boundless love, even for those who may, in the end, betray You. Your forgiveness and mercy are a gift beyond measure.

Lord, grant us the strength to become true Talmidim, disciples who eagerly follow in Your footsteps. May we be covered in Your dust, and may our lives radiate so much of Your love and grace that others are irresistibly drawn to You, like moths to a flame.

Amen.

Reachable Questions for Reflection

1. The author said, "Our modern world yearns for a meaningful connection with the divine, but not with just any god." After reading this chapter, what are some

examples you have seen as evidence of this statement in friends, loved ones, and perhaps even strangers?

2. Perhaps the one thing to which everyone in the world can agree upon is that the world is broken. What are some practical steps we, as Christians, can use to make the world different? Can you think of a neighbor or friend who may be struggling in this broken world that needs your help and influence in their life as you point them to Jesus?

3. Thinking back in your own life, have you sought a "magic formula" out of desperation for hope? What did you discover?

4. Can you think of some ways you have tried to hide from Jesus? Do you remember when he called you out of hiding? How might you use your story to help others hear the voice of Jesus beckoning them to come home?

5. In what ways do you believe the Shama might be helpful in spiritual formation today?

6. Are you dancing with the divine? Are you ready to teach others to dance?

Chapter 6

The Eternal Footprints of a Legacy
Living the Journey of Faith

The days are surely coming, says the Lord, when I will make a new covenant with the house of Israel and the house of Judah. But this is the covenant that I will make with the house of Israel after those days, says the Lord: I will put my law within them, and I will write it on their hearts, and I will be their God, and they shall be my people.[126]

Jeremiah's words give us a glimpse into such a time. Israel, once shining brightly with God's promise, had lost its glow. They used to be united, like a choir singing in perfect harmony. But after King Solomon's time, things changed. Two separate kingdoms formed: the northern one, Israel, and the southern one, Judah. These kingdoms drifted apart around 930 BCE, with different politics and beliefs.[127]

Over the years, the northern kingdom met its fate with the Assyrians in 722 BCE. Meanwhile, the southern kingdom, Judah, held on a bit longer. However, the Babylonians overtook them in 586 BCE.[128] This once proud nation, which stood as a shining

---

126. Jeremiah 31,33, NRSV.
127. Varughese, Alex. *Jeremiah 1-25: A Commentary in the Wesleyan Tradition (New Beacon Bible Commentary).* Beacon Hill Press of Kansas City, 2008.
128. Varughese, Alex. *Jeremiah 1-25: A Commentary in the Wesleyan Tradition (New Beacon Bible Commentary).* Beacon Hill Press of Kansas City, 2008.

example of God's promise, now looked defeated. But the truth is, they had strayed from God's path, just like Adam and others before them. They were distracted, sometimes worshiping other gods and only turning to God when it suited them.

But in these dark times, hope wasn't lost. A message of hope rang out, like a beautiful song on a quiet night. God's judgment was a way to bring them back, to remind them of His love. They were told of a new promise, a promise where God's words would be written on their hearts, never to be forgotten. A time where they would come together, united, full of love and faith.

God gave this promise through Jeremiah, but the people still faced hardship in Babylon for many years. And during tough times, doubt can sneak in. We're taught to pray, but sometimes, the answers might not come immediately or in the way we expect. It's in these moments that doubt tries to overshadow our faith.

From Humble Beginnings to Heaven's Champion

In our journey with faith, where doubt and hope play a delicate dance, I'm reminded of my grandfather, Frank. His story is intertwined with struggles and triumphs, embodying the spirit of resilience that runs deep in the tales from the Bible and serves as a reminder of Isaiah's words: "But those who wait on the Lord Shall renew their strength; They shall mount up with wings like eagles, they shall run and not be weary, they shall walk and not faint."[129]

Frank lived during the daunting era of the Great Depression. With only a third-grade education, life didn't offer him many privileges. To feed his family, he cut wood for mere pennies a day and worked as a tenant farmer, farming another man's land. His own father, rather than supporting him, took away the hard-earned money he made. By living in a humble one-room shack with curtains made of potato sacks, life seemed a constant uphill battle for Frank.

---

129. Isaiah 40:31 (NRSV)

Yet, the challenges didn't end there. Drafted into World War II, Frank faced the horrors of war. But every cloud has its silver lining. After returning home, he secured a job as a machine tech at a paper mill. Around this time, his wife, Thelma, became his beacon of hope and knowledge. She patiently taught him to read, using the Bible as their guide.

In one transformative moment, while he was alone in the woods, a radiant figure descended, entrusting him with a divine purpose—to preach the gospel. Overwhelmed by this vision, Frank ran from the woods, his heart ablaze with newfound passion. From modest beginnings, preaching from front porches, he became a Nazarene pastor. But, due to his limited formal education, the denominational leadership eventually forced him to step away from preaching.

While some might have seen Frank as a man who couldn't win in life or even, as he felt at times, labeled by others as a "loser," Frank's spirit was unbreakable. He never demanded respect or riches. Instead, he always said, "Here am I… Send me." His legacy was one of obedience and love.

During these trying moments, when my expectations of God lead to feelings of delay and disappointment, I am taken back to the memory of my grandfather's long days. Rising at 4:00 a.m. to start work by 5:00 a.m., he'd come home, freshen up, and visit members of his congregation. After tending to his garden and once the household was silent, he'd retreat to his den. There, kneeling before the couch, he'd pour his heart out in prayer. The depth and sincerity of his prayers were unparalleled. He'd pray for the nation, for our family, for his grandchildren, and for his modest church in Peterson, Alabama—a church that stood simple, with wooden floors, devoid of modern comforts like air-conditioning or indoor plumbing. He'd whisper, he'd shout, and he would weep. This happened nightly and for at least an hour and often more.

God used Frank in wondrous ways. All but one of Frank's children and most of his grandchildren grew up to lead dedicated

Christian lives, serving their communities. They got married, built churches, taught Sunday school, and even took up roles as ministers. Frank's legacy did not stop there. Among his seven grandchildren, all became active church members, with three entering full-time ministry. These "grandchildren of a loser," as the world might have dubbed Frank, achieved advanced degrees and served in notable leadership roles.

Frank died in a nursing home just after his ninety-first birthday, but his impact remains unwavering. His legacy of faith, from the depths of adversity, stands testament to the promise that God always sees beyond worldly labels. Frank's life is a testament that when the world might call you a "loser," God sees a faithful servant ready to answer His call.

I am confident when "grandaddy" met Jesus, he did not ask for his heavenly rewards. No, I am sure he asked, "What needs to be done?" Because that's who Frank was, a man whose legacy shines bright, even though he's gone. A man who, despite life's challenges, always believed when God said, "I will supply all thy needs."

Frank was the only person that I can say ever really mentored me. He did not sit down and read the Bible with me. He didn't give me long assignments to write theological discourses on scriptures or even require me to memorize various books of the Bible. He loved me! As I worked alongside him after the papermill shut down and he was forced to do odd jobs in the community, he would sometimes lose patience with me, but I never doubted his love. He taught things like how to cut the grass, hammer a nail, and cut a two-by-four. He taught me to measure twice and cut once, and even then, you sometimes make mistakes.

Living Generously: Frank's Legacy of Love

While I might not have inherited the knack for some tasks, the deeper, more significant lessons from him weren't about chores or skills. It was the acts born out of his unwavering love for the

Lord that left the most profound impressions on me. Often, I'd observe, sometimes closely and sometimes from afar, his perseverance in prayer—especially during moments when it felt futile.

Frank's commitment wasn't just to his faith but extended to serving everyone around him, whether they were members of his church or just neighbors in need. Despite his modest means, Frank's generosity knew no bounds. He toiled for months in his four gardens, ensuring they bore the best produce. And while the family did enjoy the fruits of his labor, the community knew the richness of Frank's heart. For just a dollar, anyone could knock on his door and pick a bag full of fresh vegetables, with Frank never asking for more. This wasn't just about food—it was a testament to Frank's endless capacity to give.

The Making of a Legacy

I share the tale of my grandfather not merely as a nostalgic memory, but as a testament to the making of legacies. The teachings my dear grandaddy believed he was imparting were often different from the profound truths I absorbed. It wasn't through his words but through our shared moments that he truly "shepherded" my spirit. Frank may never have labeled his actions as "mentoring," yet as I beheld his unyielding perseverance, as I witnessed people slight him only to be met with his grace and humility, I was deeply stirred. To observe him labor without a murmur of complaint spoke volumes to my heart.

Witnessing my grandaddy's footsteps, walking in the "dust of my Rabbi," has molded my spirit in intricate ways I am yet unraveling. Likewise, your legacy shall reverberate through your actions and daily living. Recall the Great Commission: "Go into all the world." Yet, in the original Greek, the essence is "as you go." Thus, let our lives, in every step and every breath, be that living testimony. While legacies are not accidentally shaped, neither are they formulaic. If only life had a recipe for guaranteeing that our children and grandchildren all grow up to love the Lord, love their families, and love their neighbors. The church has sometimes been guilty of portraying the Christian life as just that. It begins by praying the "sinner's prayer." Unfortunately, for some, that is the beginning and the end.

A Model of Servanthood

"Who, being in very nature God, did not consider equality with God something to be used to his own advantage; rather, he made himself nothing by taking the very nature of a servant, being made in human likeness."[130]

In our journey of faith, there exists an often-unnoticed facet of discipleship: the profound significance of mental and emotional health. As we endeavor to guide and exemplify the Christian faith for others, we invariably encounter individuals navigating various levels of brokenness. Some have endured the relentless blows of trauma, abuse, or neglect, while others wrestle with the weight of mental health challenges. Additionally, certain individuals may find themselves in need of essential life skills guidance.

Recalling the words of Philippians 2:6–7, we're reminded of Jesus' unparalleled humility: "Who, being in very nature God, did not consider equality with God something to be used to his own advantage; rather, he made himself nothing by taking the very nature of a servant, being made in human likeness." Like Jesus, who chose the path of humility despite His divine nature, we, too, must embrace the role of servants.

Frank serves as a shining model of servanthood. Throughout his life, every action he undertook was rooted in the desire to uplift others. He never aspired to climb the ranks within the church, seek promotions at work, or boast about the number of souls he led to the Lord despite his substantial impact. Frank's heart remained humble before both the Lord and his fellow human beings.

---

130. Philippians 2:6–7 (NIV)

As we strive to assist those in need, we must remain vigilant against the pitfalls of pride. It's all too easy to unintentionally condescend or become dependent on their admiration. This perilous trap, known as the "messiah complex," can lead us to view ourselves as their sole saviors. Frank, true to form, never succumbed to this temptation and maintained his love for those he served. A lasting legacy begins with humility. Just as Satan tempted Jesus in the wilderness to lift himself up, we too are vulnerable to the same temptation. A Christian legacy is never about fame, it is about servanthood. When Jesus was finally lifted up, it was upon a cross.

Addressing Mental and Emotional Health
The Overlooked Aspect of Discipleship

While we dedicate ourselves to spiritual growth, we must not neglect the critical issue of mental and emotional well-being. Discipleship brings us face-to-face with individuals grappling with profound brokenness in their lives. This may manifest as the aftermath of trauma, the scars of abuse, or the complexities of mental health issues. In some instances, individuals may require guidance in mastering fundamental life skills.

I recall a particular family within one of my congregations that required patient guidance on basic self-care routines, such as personal hygiene and clothing maintenance. Others needed support in learning how to maintain a clean and orderly living space. Initially, their gratitude for our assistance was evident.

Eventually, the alien nature of their change began to be very uncomfortable. The family's own past traumas and neglect rose to the surface, as often happens, and then they turned their anger towards those within the church who were helping. Those who were helping were able to navigate the relational perils, but it serves as a reminder that discipleship is messy and is not a straight line from brokenness to wholeness.

The Holistic Nature of Discipleship

It's important to acknowledge that discipleship extends far beyond the spiritual realm. Mental and emotional health profoundly impacts every facet of an individual's life, including the physical and spiritual aspects. Yet, discipleship has historically focused primarily on the spiritual realm, overlooking the holistic needs of individuals. Therefore, recognizing the importance of maintaining access to trusted Christian mental health professionals is paramount.

In our commitment to serve, we must not disregard our own mental health. I recommend establishing a relationship with a counselor to process our ministry encounters. We, too, can become cynical without realizing it, and the fusion of our traumas and emotional wounds with those we mentor can quickly turn toxic.

Cynicism can take root when we've experienced hurt and disappointment in our ministries. It fosters suspicion and causes us to question even the purest motives of those willing to help. Recognizing these signs is crucial to prevent spiritual burnout.

It's imperative that we confront and heal our own emotional wounds. Untreated trauma and past abuse can detrimentally affect our leadership and relationships, as well as our ability to mentor effectively.

Coping with Difficult Encounters

In the course of ministry, we must be prepared for the inevitability of challenging encounters. These encounters can serve as powerful learning experiences, and I recall one such moment from my own life—a memory I'm not proud of.

I had initiated a Celebrate Recovery ministry within our church, recognizing that this program was designed not only for addictions like alcohol or drugs but also for individuals grappling with various types of issues. One lady in our group had grown up in an environment marked by significant dysfunction. As she started to grow closer to the group, a distressing pattern emerged—she began to disrupt the relationships within it.

At one point, her frustrations led to verbal attacks directed at my wife. I admit that I didn't respond to this situation as I should have. My reaction became the focal point of the problem and ultimately led to the demise of both my personal witness and the Celebrate Recovery ministry we had established. This regrettable incident remains a dark spot in my ministry journey, one that the enemy constantly reminds me of during moments of self-doubt.

It's not uncommon to find ourselves trapped in a cycle of negative thinking or fatalism when faced with such dark moments. During these challenging times, I've learned to remind myself to surrender my burdens to the feet of Jesus. Furthermore, I've come to recognize the importance of seeking support when necessary, including scheduling sessions with a counselor if the weight of the situation becomes overwhelming.

Not Every Struggle Is a Spiritual Struggle

Maintaining access to trusted Christian mental health professionals is also important to help discern when there is a problem that is not necessarily a spiritual problem. A failure to recognize this can result in significant harm and even legal peril. I can vividly recall an incident involving a woman who was grappling with postpartum depression. She sought guidance from a pastor who repeatedly advised her that her depression was a result of a "lack of faith" and urged her to place her trust solely in God for healing. This persisted for several months. Thankfully, the pastor had a Christian psychologist within the congregation who became aware of the lady's struggles. Upon learning about her situation, the psychologist reached out to her. It was then revealed that the woman had been contemplating a tragic act—loading her children into her van and driving into the river.

The conclusion of this story serves as a poignant reminder of two important lessons. First, it underscores the inherent dangers of succumbing to the "Messiah complex," wherein we perceive ourselves as the sole saviors of those we aim to help. Second, it emphasizes that discipleship is a comprehensive and holistic process. We must be cautious not to overly spiritualize every issue we encounter as we strive to foster Christ-centered relationships within our community.

Responding to Hurt with Service

Jesus spent three years of his life pouring into twelve men. There were not many days in which they were apart. Jesus' humanity is often minimized. But, the biblical story of salvation is dependent upon the fact that Jesus was fully human and fully God. As a human, Jesus was susceptible to the same ailments and frustrations as us. When Jesus entered that upper room on their final night together to share one last meal, he knew or at least had an idea that someone would betray Him and most would abandon Him. Peter would deny Him. It was with this knowledge that Jesus stood up, removed His outer cloth, picked up a towel, and began to wash their feet.

Throughout Jesus' ministry He had been attacked and undermined. It would have been easy for Jesus to have become cynical, create a mental file that He took with Him, and pulled that file out on every new relationship, especially with those whom He knew would betray and abandon Him. But instead of picking up a file, He picked up a towel and served. He began to wash the feet of His disciples. When people serve, it reveals who they are. When we are served, it reveals who we are. Frank, my grandfather, exemplified this approach throughout his life. Despite facing moments of betrayal and abandonment, he never allowed these experiences to overshadow his profound love for both the people he served and his devotion to the Lord. Frank's legacy is a testament to the transformative power of serving others in the shape of the cross—humility, love, and unwavering commitment. That's a legacy.

Guarding Against Reductionism in Our Faith

If we are not careful, we can become reductionistic of God, our faith, and our legacy. When we do this, we break the first commandment, which is, "You shall have no other Gods before me."[82] Reductionism is the perspective that suggests that explanations at a higher level of organization can be fully explained by lower-level explanations. It's closely related to the idea that everything can be reduced to the laws of physics. While reducing complex ideas to their simplest forms has merit for the purposes of better understanding, it also risks making things seem too simple and causes us to miss important things that happen when different parts work together in more complicated ways.

When we try to explain God in human terms, we often simplify Him to something we can understand. However, this is a problem because God is beyond our complete comprehension. God is irreducible. Any reduction of God by humans is not God. While we may think of idolatry as worshiping statues made of stone or wood, in today's world, it's not always that obvious. An idol can be anything or anyone we turn to for happiness and purpose in life instead of relying on God.

We should never try to diminish God to anything less than what we see in Jesus. God is fully revealed in the person of Jesus, even though this truth can be challenging to accept. When God took on human form in Jesus, His own creation sought to kill Him, which is the scandal in the story of the cross. Jesus did not die so we could be happy. Jesus did not tell the disciples, "Follow me and leave a lasting legacy." Even our legacy can become an idol. The cross is the only way to this salvation. It's not about saying a special prayer or going to church; it's about the merciful and gracious act of Jesus on that hill they called "the skull." *Salus per gratiam per fidem.* ("Salvation by grace through faith.") Any other path leads to idolatry.

More Art Than Science

I frequently use metaphors rooted in art forms for a specific purpose. While science can offer insights into the transformative nature of Christian spiritual growth (for a deeper exploration, Joseph Chilton Pearce's *The Biology of Transcendence* is recommended), the intricacies of relationships nurtured within the Christian faith defy simplification into a mere three or four-step process leading to Christian identity. It doesn't neatly fit into a ten-step formula for guaranteed success. I've had the privilege of observing parents greatly admired for their unwavering faith, both within and beyond the church, who were profoundly saddened when their adult children chose to depart from the church and their Christian beliefs.

Conversely, I've known individuals whose parents never set foot in a church, openly professed agnosticism, and yet they emerged as steadfast followers of the Christian faith. Reflecting on the life of Jesus provides another profound example. Jesus, the Son of God, had twelve disciples and drew crowds of thousands. However, among His closest followers, Peter denied knowing Him, and Judas betrayed Him. As He hung on the cross, the only disciple explicitly mentioned was John, the beloved disciple. From the cross, Jesus entrusted the care of His mother, Mary, to John.[131] If God had coerced these relationships, the profound significance of the crucifixion would have been rendered meaningless.

While it's certainly essential to prepare for mentoring and discipleship, we must never forget the element of free will. Regardless of how meticulously we plan or how extensive our knowledge is, we must ultimately place our trust in the work of the Holy Spirit. There is an organic aspect to mentoring. Our primary duty is to faithfully obey the Lord, involving prayer, discernment, and a deep degree of self-awareness. It's crucial to recognize that mentoring and discipleship are not exact sciences;

---

131. John 19:25–27 (NRSV)

they require patient attunement to the Holy Spirit and to the unique journey of each mentee.

In recent decades, there has been a noticeable trend of emphasizing decisions over discipleship within the realm of faith. The rush to quantify our "spiritual progress," engage in spiritual competitions for souls, and tally up salvations has inadvertently led to a reduction of salvation to a mere prayer of forgiveness. Yet, we must remember that repentance, the act of turning around and changing one's ways, is a vital component of salvation. It's challenging to suggest that discipleship begins at the point of repentance, as God's nurturing and pursuit of His "lost sheep" commences at the calvary itself.[132] We might liken repentance to the moment when "scales are removed from our eyes," allowing us to see Jesus more clearly and begin following Him.[133] However, it is crucial not to oversimplify the Christian faith as a one-time decision. Discipleship loses its significance if we reduce faith to a singular decision. Even discipleship can become an idol when we reduce it.

True legacies are not built upon a solitary decision but are forged through daily choices. Even momentary decisions, where we steadfastly resist the allure of shortcuts and the reduction of faith to a mere formula, contribute to the lasting legacy of faith. Each day presents opportunities to live out our faith, to make choices that align with our beliefs, and to continuously follow Jesus on the journey of discipleship.

Divine Connections: How God Works Through Faithful Individuals

God accomplishes remarkable deeds through individuals who exhibit faithfulness and obedience. I'm reminded of one such instance from my own ministry experience. During my preparations for ministry, I served on the staff of a church. As a

132. Luke 15:3–7 (NRSV)
133. Acts 9:17–18 (NRSV)

minister-in-training, my wife and I were tasked by denominational leadership within our district to establish and lead a district
IMPACT (Immediate Personal Action for Christ Today) Team.
We were blessed with an amazingly talented group of teens who
lived for the Lord. We traveled around churches in the Southeast
doing outreach and service within communities and performed
later that same evening at a local church. We had no idea that
God would use one young man in the future and his own faithfulness would connect him to a legacy that stretched to the other
side of the world.

Rev. J. O. McClurkan's Vision

Rev. J. O. McClurkan established the Pentecostal Mission in
Nashville, Tennessee, in the late 1890s.[134] This holiness-based,
missions-focused group sent out missionaries soon after. Rev. J.
O. McClurkan established the Pentecostal Mission in Nashville,
Tennessee, in the late 1890s.[135] Leona Gardner was one of those
early missionaries who went into the second group in 1902.[136] The
group, the size unknown, was on the way to Colombia in South
America when they stopped at Trinidad, a city in south-central
Cuba. They never made it to Colombia. During the first year in
Cuba, the leader died. Others returned home that year.

Three years later, the last couple left Cuba, and Leona was
alone with no colleagues for support. Leona means "lioness,"
and she needed the strength of a lion to endure life as a single
woman in Cuba. She adopted a "son," Jorgé, who was orphaned
as a three-month-old infant. She raised him as her very own child,
making certain that he received a good education.

---

134. Della Hines Newman, *By the Grace of God: The Life of Grace
Prescott* (Kansas City, KS: Nazarene Publishing House, 2001).
135. Della Hines Newman, *By the Grace of God: The Life of Grace
Prescott* (Kansas City, KS: Nazarene Publishing House, 2001).
136. Della Hines Newman, *By the Grace of God: The Life of Grace
Prescott* (Kansas City, KS: Nazarene Publishing House, 2001).

Leona the Lioness's Journey

In those days, women in ministry were not always accepted. But in 1915, the Pentecostal Mission merged with the Church of the Nazarene, which accepted women in ministry. She gladly became a Nazarene. But in 1920, the Church of the Nazarene (C/N) decided to close Cuba as a mission field. But Leona, the lioness, chose to stay, supporting herself by teaching. In fact, she stayed for a total of twenty-five years, with only three furloughs. When Leona moved to Guatemala, the mission she had started closed and remained so for eighteen years. She retired in 1938 after thirty-six years in mission service.[137] When Leona died in 1944, the C/N still had not officially reopened the work in Cuba.[138] But this is not the end of the story.

A Legacy Continues: The Prescotts' Arrival

In 1945, the C/N sent Lyle and Grace Prescott as missionaries to Cuba. Frustrated at first in finding a place to restart the church, Lyle decided to move to the city of Trinidad.[139] On the train to this location, they met a Cuban man, well-dressed, who spoke English. He asked what these non-Cubans were doing in his country. When he learned they were missionaries, he said, "My mother was a missionary."[140] In the providence of God, this man was Jorgé, Leona's adopted son. He and the Prescotts were thrilled. Jorgé took them to Trinidad and helped them to get settled and to make a connection with the work of his mother.[141]

---

137. Della Hines Newman, *By the Grace of God: The Life of Grace Prescott* (Kansas City, KS: Nazarene Publishing House, 2001).
138. Della Hines Newman, *By the Grace of God: The Life of Grace Prescott* (Kansas City, KS: Nazarene Publishing House, 2001).
139. Della Hines Newman, *By the Grace of God: The Life of Grace Prescott* (Kansas City, KS: Nazarene Publishing House, 2001).
140. Della Hines Newman, *By the Grace of God: The Life of Grace Prescott* (Kansas City, KS: Nazarene Publishing House, 2001).
141. Della Hines Newman, *By the Grace of God: The Life of Grace Prescott* (Kansas City, KS: Nazarene Publishing House, 2001).

The Next Chapter: A Musician's Journey

The Prescotts had a great ministry in Cuba. They moved to Havana, the capital city. Other missionaries came to join them, and the Lord's church grew in Cuba. But in 1959, when Fidel Castro became Cuba's leader, all the Nazarene missionaries were eventually forced to leave, either moving to other countries or going home.[142] But that is not the end of the story.

From Cuba to Russia: The Rus Family

At this time in Cuba's history, there was a gifted musician by the name of Mario Rus. He moved to Russia to study music, finding it easier due to the communist connection between Castro's Cuba and the Soviet Union. While studying there, he met and married a Russian lady by the name of Lena. Later, they had a daughter and named her Irina.[143]

A New Faith in a New Land

When Mario's studies were completed, he decided to move back to Cuba. Once there, Mario came into contact with the Church of the Nazarene.[144] By the grace of God, Mario and Lena became Christians through the people called Nazarenes. Later, they decided to return to Russia, and naturally, they looked for a Church of the Nazarene. They found one in Moscow, the capital city.[145]

---

142. Della Hines Newman, *By the Grace of God: The Life of Grace Prescott* (Kansas City, KS: Nazarene Publishing House, 2001).
143. Della Hines Newman, *By the Grace of God: The Life of Grace Prescott* (Kansas City, KS: Nazarene Publishing House, 2001).
144. Della Hines Newman, *By the Grace of God: The Life of Grace Prescott* (Kansas City, KS: Nazarene Publishing House, 2001).
145. Della Hines Newman, *By the Grace of God: The Life of Grace Prescott* (Kansas City, KS: Nazarene Publishing House, 2001).

Answering the Call: Mario's Ministry

As the couple attended and worked in the church, Mario felt a call to preach. While studying to become a pastor, he worked two jobs, and Mario was one of the first men to be ordained in Russia. Later, Lena died, leaving him without his Russian wife. But he chose not to return to his home country but remain in Russia with his daughter, Irina.[146] But that's not the end of the story.

Across Borders: Sergey's Journey

In Ukraine, there was a young man by the name of Sergey, who became an alcoholic, one of the many young people who become addicts. By the age of twenty, he had been an addict for six years. His family took him to one of the Nazarene rehabilitation centers. He rebelled at first, as he was not a willing client. He broke the rules, smoking and inhaling glue. But at long last, the Holy Spirit broke through his hard heart, and this young adult surrendered to Christ.[147]

Answering the Call to Ministry

Sergey had a gift for music. He enjoyed playing the guitar, singing, and even writing his own songs, blessing the other men in the rehab and in the church he attended. After some time, Sergey felt God was calling him to the ministry, and he began his pastoral training. One of his classes took him to Russia. And while there, he met Pastor Mario's daughter, Irina. As Cupid has a way of doing, his arrows hit both of their hearts. Sergey and Irina fell in love and married. And together, they planned for a life of ministry.[148]

---

146. Parker, J. Fred, and Jerald D. Johnson. *Mission to the World: Me Through 1985.* Kansas City, KS: Nazarene Publishing House, 1988.
147. Parker, J. Fred, and Jerald D. Johnson. *Mission to the World: Me Through 1985.* Kansas City, KS: Nazarene Publishing House, 1988.
148. Parker, J. Fred, and Jerald D. Johnson. *Mission to the World: Me Through 1985.* Kansas City, KS: Nazarene Publishing House, 1988.

A Message of Hope in Moldova and Ukraine

To the west of Ukraine is the smaller country of Moldova, squeezed between Ukraine and Romania. It's an extremely poor country, maybe the poorest in all of Europe. Many adults leave the country searching for work elsewhere, often leaving their children behind in Moldova. As a result, many of the kids and youth become addicts at a young age, and some are kidnapped and become part of human trafficking.[149]

God's Plan Unfolds: Sergey and Irina's Commission

The Church of the Nazarene decided to go to Moldova to give the people there the message of hope and Good News. And when they looked around for missionaries, they felt God was placing His hand on Sergey and Irina. The Church of the Nazarene in Ukraine commissioned and sent them as regional missionaries in 2010.[150]

A New Chapter Begins: Jacob's Response to the Syrian Crisis

One of the young men who had been a part of the IMPACT team grew up and pursued a pastoral education at a college in Nashville. Later, he ventured to Europe to pursue his doctorate. It was during this time that he met a young woman overseas, and they eventually tied the knot and welcomed a child into their lives.[151]

Compassion in the Midst of Crisis

Around 2015, the Syrian civil war was devastating countless lives. In September 2015, a heart-wrenching photograph circulated

---

149. Parker, J. Fred, and Jerald D. Johnson. *Mission to the World: Me Through 1985.* Kansas City, KS: Nazarene Publishing House, 1988.
150. Kathy Mowry, lecture at Pastors Conference, Nashville, TN, March 6, 2016.
151. Kathy Mowry, lecture at Pastors Conference, Nashville, TN, March 6, 2016.

worldwide depicting the lifeless body of a three-year-old Syrian boy, Alan Kurdi, washed ashore on a beach in Turkey. This tragic image served as a poignant symbol of the refugee crisis stemming from the Syrian conflict, bringing global attention to the ongoing war and the plight of Syrian refugees.[152]

The picture resonated deeply with Jacob and his wife, as they had a son of similar age. In response, they made the decision to move to the region to provide aid during the refugee crisis, extending their efforts to areas including Moldova and Ukraine.[153]

The grand tapestry of God's plan spans across the pages of history, interconnecting our stories when willing souls answer His call. This narrative traces its origins back over a century to the faithful commitment of one individual. Each individual in these stories was earnestly following God's will and purpose for their lives, subsequently impacting the lives of those around them.

"In our journey of discipleship and mentoring, it's crucial to remember the profound wisdom found in these words: 'A warrior asks a god for advice and the god replies, 'If the only way you can conquer me is through love, then and there I will gladly be conquered.'"[154] These narratives of ordinary people living ordinary lives serve as a compelling contemporary illustration of discipleship and mentoring. While plans hold significance, it is crucial to recognize that the most profound impact emanates from our obedience and unwavering faithfulness to God's divine plan. They were ordinary people when God called them to serve and serve; they gladly did. God is not looking for mighty men and women, nor does He require people with a Ph.D. in Theology or even biblical scholars. What He seeks are servants' hearts.

---

152. Kathy Mowry, lecture at Pastors Conference, Nashville, TN, March 6, 2016.

153. Kathy Mowry, lecture at Pastors Conference, Nashville, TN, March 6, 2016.

154. Neale Donald Walsch, *Conversations with God: An Uncommon Dialogue, Book 1* (New York: G.P. Putnam's Sons, 1996

The Importance of Consistency

I've encountered many leaders who possessed remarkable gifts. They exuded intelligence, charisma, and had a way with words that captivated their audience. However, despite these talents, they often fell short in one critical aspect: consistency. It's possible that they struggled with setting boundaries and inadvertently overpromised or genuinely intended to keep their commitments. Nevertheless, these leaders faced a credibility issue, as they consistently overpromised and underdelivered. Whether it was a scheduled lunch with a client, a promise to attend their daughter's softball game, or a commitment to dinner with their spouse, the specifics mattered less than the overarching issue. Due to their inconsistency, the impact and influence of these leaders on those around them were dampened, and the full potential of their kingdom impact remained unrealized.

This situation brings to mind a timeless parable that has been passed down through generations. It tells of a person with an empty jar and a supply of marbles. Each day, a marble is placed in the jar, symbolizing a day lived. As time passes, the jar fills with marbles, representing the accumulation of shared experiences, trust, and positive interactions with others. In the realm of relationships and trust-building, the more marbles in the jar, the stronger the foundation of trust and connection. It signifies consistent reliability, showing up, and building a history of positive interactions.

Conversely, any breach of trust or negative interactions can be likened to removing marbles from the jar, depleting the trust painstakingly built over time. The Marble Jar Story serves as a reminder of the paramount importance of consistency, reliability, and positive actions in the context of trust and relationship-building. It encourages individuals to contemplate how their daily choices and interactions impact the trust and connections they forge with others.

Once again, the stories of the lives of Frank, J.O. McClurkin, Leona the Lioness, Mario, Sergey, and the countless unknown others who mentored them echo through eternity and their reverberations continue today.[155] If not for their unwavering consistency, it is worth imagining how those stories might have unfolded differently and how our own lives would be irrevocably changed as a result.

It's worth emphasizing that we should never try to limit or simplify God's vastness. These legacies we create, filled with heartwarming stories and touching illustrations that bring tears of joy to our eyes, serve as beautiful reminders. The idea that someday someone might share a story of how our faithfulness, obedience, and unwavering love for them and the Lord impacted their lives is indeed an admirable aspiration. However, as inspiring as these stories are, they alone lack the power to bring about transformation. They ignite our imagination and motivate us to action, but without God going before us, without the work of the Holy Spirit, their impact tends to fade quickly, like a feather gently descending in a quiet forest. When we attempt to diminish God's majesty, we inadvertently reduce His influence, and our efforts may ultimately be in vain.[156]

If you permit me to delve a bit deeper into the theological realm without becoming overly philosophical, I firmly believe in practicality. However, it's crucial for us to grasp the theological foundation behind our actions and their consequences. We shouldn't compromise our theological core principles simply because a particular method appears effective.

As I have emphasized multiple times, as participants in the kingdom of God, every action we take is seen through the lens of Jesus' crucifixion. Jesus didn't endure the cross because it was practical or convenient. His sacrifice held no practicality for anyone

155. Della Hines Newman, *By the Grace of God: The Life of Grace Prescott* (Kansas City, KS: Nazarene Publishing House, 2001).
156. Psalm 127:1 (ESV)

except the Roman Empire and the religious elite, whose authority was challenged. Our actions must align with God's ways and reflect His character because we bear His image and serve as witnesses to His nature. Ultimately, the point of Metanoia (transformation) is wholeness.[157] One cannot be made whole with partial truths; and reductionism is the result of embracing half-truths.

Alan Hirsch says:

> Alongside the eclipsing of God, there has been a corresponding loss of the whole due to a focusing on the parts. In other words, we have lost a sense of the big story that makes sense of all our little stories. It is this loss of wholeness that contributes to the eclipse, concealing and alienating us from the truth of the one God.[158]

In its original sense, the term "heresy" does not imply that someone is incorrect or has embraced a false belief. Instead, it merely signifies a specific truth or doctrine that has been isolated from its genuine and comprehensive context and is then regarded as if it represents the entirety of truth.[159] The poet Rumi lamented this shattering of truth:

> *The Truth was a mirror in the hands of God.*
> *It fell and broke into pieces. Everybody took a piece of it and they*
> *looked at it and thought they had the truth.*[160]

---

157. Hirsch, Alan; Kelly, Rob. *Metanoia: How God Radically Transforms People, Churches, and Organizations From the Inside Out* (p. 21). 100 Movements Publishing. Kindle Edition.

158. Dean, Kenda Creasy. *Almost Christian* (p. 12). Oxford University Press. Kindle Edition.

159. Hirsch, Alan; Nelson, Mark. *Reframation: Seeing God, People, and Mission Through Reenchanted Frames* (p. 48). 100 Movements Publishing. Kindle Edition

160. Hirsch, Alan; Nelson, Mark. *Reframation: Seeing God, People, and Mission Through Reenchanted Frames* (p. 49). 100 Movements Publishing. Kindle Edition.

Heresy is not confined solely to the realm of theology and religion. It permeates various domains of knowledge, affecting nearly every facet of human understanding. In theological, political, or sociological spheres, heresy manifests when complex ideas are distilled and compressed into a singular, overarching "ideology." This ideology often becomes the lens through which insiders interpret their world and formulate their actions.

Beyond theology, even within the realms of science and philosophy, heresy takes root when knowledge becomes overly specialized and fragmented. This specialization often leads to conflicts among different specialties, each vying for the claim of ultimate correctness. Philosopher E. F. Schumacher laments this trend, quoting psychiatrist Viktor Frankl, who notes that the true peril lies not in scientists' specialization but in their presumption of totality.[161] The danger, in essence, lies in specialists attempting to generalize their expertise. Today's nihilism is cloaked under the guise of reductionism, where everything is reduced to mere "nothing-but-ness."[162]

"The consequences of reductionism are profound. It can engender an unhealthy fixation on a single idea, giving rise to the monomaniac or fanatic."[163] Fanatics typically lack empathy, humility, and a holistic view of humanity. A stark example of this phenomenon can be seen in contemporary suicide bombers who become radicalized through an obsessive focus on a reductionist

---

161. Hirsch, Alan; Nelson, Mark. *Reframation: Seeing God, People, and Mission Through Reenchanted Frames* (p. 49). 100 Movements Publishing. Kindle Edition.

162. Hirsch, Alan; Nelson, Mark. *Reframation: Seeing God, People, and Mission Through Reenchanted Frames* (p. 49). 100 Movements Publishing. Kindle Edition.

163. Hirsch, Alan; Nelson, Mark. *Reframation: Seeing God, People, and Mission Through Reenchanted Frames* (p. 49). 100 Movements Publishing. Kindle Edition.

Jihadist ideology.[164] In their fanaticism, they sever meaningful relationships and lose perspective.[165]

Let's not assume that ideological fanaticism is limited to specific groups; you can simply look at the ongoing division in the United States as an example. The rigid "either/or" ideologies of fervent conservatives and the elitist attitudes of liberal elites obstruct the capacity to recognize truth in one another, let alone interact as fellow human beings. This reductionist mindset even infiltrates Christian circles.

Once more, Alan Hirsh calls us out:

> Most conservative evangelicals, they do not believe that God is a lively character and a real agent, because they've got God all packaged up into sustained systematic explanations. And if you consider most theological progressives, they don't believe that God is a real character and a lively agent either, because they really believe that God has no hands but our hands. [166]

Moralistic Therapeutic Deism

In conclusion of my point regarding reductionism, let me emphasize my point by referring to Kendra Casey Dean, the author of *Almost Christian*. She argues that the theology embraced by the next generation can often be described as a somewhat loveless form of Christianity, which she terms MTD (Moralistic Therapeutic Deism) because it is the only Christianity they know.[167]

164. Hirsch, Alan; Nelson, Mark. *Reframation: Seeing God, People, and Mission Through Reenchanted Frames* (p. 49). 100 Movements Publishing. Kindle Edition.

165. Hirsch, Alan; Nelson, Mark. *Reframation: Seeing God, People, and Mission Through Reenchanted Frames* (p. 49). 100 Movements Publishing. Kindle Edition.

166. Hirsch, Alan; Nelson, Mark. *Reframation: Seeing God, People, and Mission Through Reenchanted Frames* (p. 49). 100 Movements Publishing. Kindle Edition.

167. Dean, Kenda Creasy. *Almost Christian* (p. 12). Oxford University Press. Kindle Edition.

It is essentially the faith that has been modeled for them.[168] We have reduced God's relationship with humanity as one in which God desires us to be happy and to be good people who are kind, but beyond that hope for humanity, God has little to no involvement in our daily lives. This is the result of faith, which has reduced abundant life to happiness, and the penultimate goal of salvation is to go to heaven. Such a faith has no consequential impact on the here and now. If we want to reach the next generations, we must offer them a holistic faith that offers more than future rewards. A holistic faith will encompass and integrate all aspects of their lives. If we can model a faith that is more than what one individual believes but is interconnected to God, each other, and the world around us, that is a God that will fit like a hand in the glove to this interconnected generation. Remember the Icon of Rublev? This is essentially an invitation for humanity to join with the trinity in their divine dance of love.

Though He Slay Me, I Will Serve Him

When it comes to young people finding their rhythm in the divine dance of life, I can't help but think of another remarkable young lady whose journey my wife, Lisa, and I had the privilege of witnessing. She was a truly gifted individual—a singer, an artist, and incredibly bright. Her parents beamed with pride, and her little sister, with her jet-black hair and cherubic cheeks, always wore a beaming smile. Every Sunday, you'd find them on the front row while their dad, the Sunday school superintendent, would take the stage to make announcements and guide the service.

As the years passed, she transitioned into her teenage years and found herself on the same IMPACT team as the young man whose story I shared earlier, the one who ventured to Moldova to rescue refugees. College beckoned, and she pursued a degree in English composition, refining her writing skills along the way.

---

168. Dean, Kenda Creasy. *Almost Christian* (p. 12). Oxford University Press. Kindle Edition.

Eventually, she became a master poet, earning a scholarship for graduate school, where she delved deeper into the realm of creative writing—and oh, how creatively she wrote.

But then, just before the onset of the COVID-19 era, life dealt her a cruel blow. She was diagnosed with an extraordinarily rare form of tongue cancer, a condition that doctors admitted they had never encountered in someone so young. Typically, this was the kind of cancer they associated with septuagenarian or octogenarian men who had spent their lives smoking and using tobacco.

Over the course of a grueling year, she endured rounds of chemotherapy and radiation. She emerged from that crucible with substantial weight loss, a vanished appetite, and a feeding tube as a companion, only to discover that, despite her valiant battle, the cancer still persisted. In her own words:

> Got news yesterday: my biopsy revealed I still have cancer. After all the harsh poison and treatment, after all the prayer and trust, it stands as persistent disease. The decisions I have to make in the coming days hardly feel like I have a choice at all. Immunotherapy or reconstructive tongue surgery. The outcomes are usually grim either way. I've grown exhausted in this illness, in prayer, belief, and faith. I suffer daily and have now for over a year. I am well acquainted with pain. Crying, moaning, and even yelling out for help are part of who I am. And there's nothing I can do except trust I'm where I'm meant to be. Maybe it'll be better tomorrow. God's plan is the best, no matter what. Love works for my good. Even though it hurts. Literally. Every day. So much. I often wish I could've gotten a cancer that didn't affect my eating, drinking, speech, and singing. Like, anywhere else! Please! Not my tongue/throat.
>
> More than likely, if I opt for the surgery to try and remove the cancer, my quality of life will take a hit. My speech and eating will never be the same. Communication will be harder for me (it's already not ideal). I may not speak at all. I probably won't

sing again, which absolutely shatters me. And it is common to be on a feeding tube for life. I'm a young person, so you can imagine all the dreams of a husband and children and just what we consider to be kind of a normal routine—all that gets blurry when you're staring at such a monster.

Dreams of health, travel, my writing. I'll be okay. I'll figure out how to dream new dreams. I won't be alone on this road. I have good support. I just wish things could be different. Perhaps a surprise of better health awaits me. I won't say a miracle: I'm already a miracle, and so are you. If you've been praying for a miracle in my life, consider it answered. I've always been a miracle. You have, too. If you've been asking for healing, right now, the answer is apparently no. Maybe it'll come later. I've believed as much as I could for my cancer to be gone. Tried to be positive and have good energy. I didn't stress. I focused on love taking care of me."

Thanks for praying and believing with me. God could've taken it all away at any moment, I know. I never doubt that. Even now. But love has a reason. My faith was untouchable. It still is, though it's being rocked. What a journey! I've learned so much. I thought I'd be healed today instead of typing this. But I'm not. We don't always get what we want. But I know God created me to glorify Him. I was always going to get cancer. I was going to endure a lot of suffering. Then, it wasn't going to go away after treatment. This is my story; this is my song. There's still hope. I'll still praise Him. I'm just so tired today after the news settled in. It takes effort to hope, and yeah, I've grown weary. I'm human, and it happens.[169]

She made the brave decision to undergo surgery, a procedure that required the removal of her tongue along with the cancer. Even amid the ongoing COVID-19 pandemic, she and her mother embarked on over a hundred-mile journey, enduring two nights in a hotel just to receive specialized treatment. Over the course of time, they spent over fifty nights in a hotel in Birmingham, Alabama, and thanks to God's provision, they never paid for a

---

169. Diana Reaves blog post, March 12, 2020

single night—a shining example of the kingdom of God breaking into the darkest nights. Eventually, she received the long-awaited news that she was in the clear. She learned to speak again, adapted to specific dietary restrictions, and gradually reintroduced solid foods into her life. She even graced her home with snippets of song, filling the air with her beautiful voice. Upon her return to the church after the COVID-19 hiatus, she was met with warm embraces and the love of her congregation.

In 2022, she scheduled a routine checkup, only to receive the devastating news that the cancer had returned. The doctors requested her presence a week later to discuss a plan. She returned home after that appointment. However, a few days later, I received an early morning text from her father. Diana had passed away in July of that same year. At just thirty-five years old, she possessed the faith of a saint many times her age.

While I never had the privilege of meeting Mother Teresa, I imagine that Diana bore a striking resemblance to a young version of her. Diana exuded shalom, embodying a holistic faith in a God who filled her to completion. She was truly holy, unlike anyone else I have ever known. Her impact extended to her doctors, the nurses who cared for her, and everyone who had the privilege of crossing her path. The day Diana left this world, we lost a saint. "Though he slay me, yet will I hope in him; I will surely defend my ways to his face."[170]

As we loosen our death grip on life, we are freed in amazing ways to truly live—to encounter the presence of the living God in the here and now. When we do, we might just discover that some of the darkest places become thin places or perhaps we will discover that the floor of our living room is a thin place, and even the bedside of a dying loved one, because we know that just on the other side of death is resurrection. If only we can find the courage to embrace such a faith. "Now may the God of peace himself sanctify you completely and may your whole spirit and

---

170. Job 13:15 (NIV)

soul and body be kept blameless at the coming of our Lord Jesus Christ."[171]

We may never know in this lifetime the extent of our fingerprints on the lives around us and through the arc of God's plan. The tapestry of stories that span generations and continents, all woven together by the common thread of faith and unwavering commitment to God's divine plan, drive home the point that there is no age limit on legacy. A legacy that began with the Prescotts continues to touch lives today in places they could have never planned and certainly never dreamed the brush strokes of their lives would touch.

End of Chapter 6 Summary:
Leaving Eternal Footprints of a Legacy

Sometimes, the impact of people's lives resembles a grand painting, where those used by God in mighty ways become the subjects of myth and legend. It's not that the facts are distorted, but rather the brush strokes used to depict how God worked through them become bold and sweeping, omitting the intricate details that compose the broader tapestry of their stories. In this way, their narratives assume larger-than-life proportions and rightfully earn them the status of faith heroes. However, it's vital to remember that they didn't embark on their journeys with aspirations of greatness; they were merely faithful to God's call. They were ordinary individuals, much like you and me—just like my grandfather Frank, just like Diana, just like the Prescotts.

The irony of a lasting legacy is that it remains elusive when it's our primary pursuit. Our obedience to God's call stems from a heart filled with gratitude and a commitment to our covenant relationship with Him. We don't obey to carve out a name for ourselves. Such intentions reduce our legacy to a human-made creation. The most profound legacies can only be crafted by the

---

171. 1 Thessalonians 5:23 (ESV)

divine hands of God. Only He can breathe life into these legacies; anything else is but a lifeless idol.

Reaching the next generation doesn't necessitate the possession of PhDs or the presence of impressive theologians capable of crafting grand commentaries echoing through the halls of academia. Across these interconnected narratives, a clear and resounding theme emerges when individuals wholeheartedly commit to following God's calling with unwavering consistency and dedication; their lives become a living testament to the transformative power of faith and love. Their impact resonates in the lives of others, reflecting the intricate brushwork of God's divine plan.

Principles to Living the Journey of Faith

Principle 1: Embrace the Unexpected

One of the central themes in the stories shared is the unexpected turns that life can take. Embrace the idea that God's plan often unfolds in ways we can't predict. Be open to new opportunities, even if they seem unrelated to your current path. Like the Prescotts who ended up in Cuba or Mario Rus who found faith in Russia, be willing to venture into the unknown, trusting that God's providence is at work.

Principle 2: Cultivate Consistency and Trust

The concept of consistency and trust-building, illustrated by the Marble Jar Story, is crucial in our relationships with others and with God. Strive to be consistent in your actions, promises, and commitments. Just as marbles accumulate in a jar over time, trust is built through a history of positive interactions. This principle applies to both our earthly relationships and our relationship with God. Maintain consistency in your faith journey, even in the face of challenges, and trust that God is faithful in His promises.

Principle 3: Guard Against Reductionism

In a world where ideologies and beliefs can become overly simplified and reduced, it's essential to guard against reductionism in theology and life. Seek a holistic faith that encompasses all aspects of your life and reflects the complexity of God's character. Remember that God's plan is vast and multifaceted, and our faith should align with His ways, not reduce them to narrow perspectives. As you live out your faith, be mindful of the dangers of reducing God's majesty and influence in your life.

By embracing the unexpected, cultivating consistency and trust, and guarding against reductionism, you can embark on a faith journey that reflects the stories shared in this chapter. These principles will help you navigate the twists and turns of life while staying grounded in your faith and aligned with God's divine plan.

A Prayer for Leaving Eternal Footprints of a Legacy and Living the Journey of Faith

Father, we beseech You never to let our salvation slip from our view. Ignite the flames of our initial love for You and instill within us an enduring passion for relentlessly pursuing Your divine purpose. May our lives, words, actions, and our entire existence be used in ways that align with Your grand design for humanity.

Grant us the wisdom to hold fast to the wisdom of St. Irenaeus, who declared that the glory of God is fully realized in a vibrant and alive humanity. We acknowledge that You are the very essence of life, akin to the name You unveiled to Moses: Yah ("as we inhale") Weh ("as we exhale"). It serves as a perpetual reminder that You are never farther away than a single breath.

Lord, we humbly seek Your forgiveness for the times when we've sought shortcuts and attempted to distill Your will and guidance into mere self-help manuals, bypassing the patient ferment of time. We thank You for your unwavering faithfulness to us, even when we fall short of Your perfect will.

In Your holy name, we pray.
Amen.

Reachable Questions for Reflection

1. Think about individuals in your own life who have left a lasting mark through their faithful service to the Lord and love for others. How have these people impacted your life and the lives of those around them?

2. Reflect on moments in your life when mental health challenges may have affected your ability to serve the Lord or engage in discipleship. How did you navigate this journey, and what did you learn from it? Consider how your experiences can be used to support others who may be facing similar struggles.

3. Consider how you can assist families or individuals who may lack basic life skills, such as hygiene and cleanliness. What strategies can you employ to offer help without dehumanizing or judging them? How can you approach this with empathy and respect?

4. Explore your own experiences with maintaining healthy boundaries and any struggles with a "Messiah complex" in the context of mentoring or ministry. How did you address these issues, and what lessons have you learned about setting boundaries and avoiding burnout?

5. Share your insights on dealing with personal attacks when mentoring and discipling others. What healthy strategies can be employed to respond to misplaced personal attacks in a constructive manner?

6. Discuss your understanding of "holistic faith" based on Jeff's explanation in the chapter. How do you see faith encompassing various aspects of life, including mental health and daily living?

7. Reflect on the forge of your own faith. In what ways are you currently serving God faithfully for His purpose in your life? How do you envision your legacy taking shape in the future?

8. Offer your thoughts and insights on "Moralistic Therapeutic Deism (MTD)" as described by Jeff. What are your observations about this prevailing theology among the next generation, and how do you believe it impacts their faith and discipleship?

Chapter 7

Unlocking Consequential Faith
Discovering the Final Key

When Jesus saw his ministry drawing huge crowds, he climbed a hillside. Those who were apprenticed to him, the committed, climbed with him. Arriving at a quiet place, he sat down and taught his climbing companions."[172]

Not everyone embarks on the same spiritual journey. Not everyone will be willing to make the climb. Notice that Jesus left the huge crowds, and He climbed the hillside. He sat down and taught His climbing companions. While we lament those who refuse to climb, the stark reality is not everyone will be committed enough to the journey to make the climb. The path may be too steep, some may not be ready emotionally or physically. We talked about the role of mental health in discipleship in the last chapter.

The Comparison Trap

While it is easy to judge those who cannot or will not make the climb, do not. That is a distraction from your own journey. The enemy loves to catch us in the comparison trap. Spiritual comparison, often referred to as the "comparison trap," is a common struggle that many individuals face in their faith journeys. It involves measuring one's spiritual life, experiences, or progress against that of others. While it may seem harmless, spiritual

---

172. Matthew 5:1–2 (MSG)

comparison can lead to various pitfalls and challenges within one's faith. Let's explore some of these pitfalls:

1. Inadequacy and Discouragement:

When individuals compare themselves to others who seem to have a more vibrant or seemingly "perfect" spiritual life, it can lead to feelings of inadequacy. They may feel discouraged, thinking they will never measure up to the perceived standards set by others. This sense of inadequacy can hinder their spiritual growth.

During my time planting churches, I encountered a family facing significant challenges that were readily apparent. Among them was a young man who was grappling with severe obesity while simultaneously experiencing an identity crisis. He openly identified as pansexual. The family dynamics were complex, with his mother and father having gone through multiple separations, divorces, and remarriages. To add to the complexity, their home was filled with numerous animals that roamed freely, leaving behind urine and feces wherever they pleased. The lack of proper training for these animals resulted in a pervasive odor that not only clung to their home but also became a part of their daily lives.

Upon their arrival at the church, it became evident that no one was eager to sit near this family. The discomfort and reluctance to welcome them were palpable, at least from my perspective. What struck me as ironic was that I was well aware of the struggles faced by many congregants within the church community. While this particular family's sins and challenges were on full display for all to see, it occurred to me that some of those who deemed them unworthy or unwelcome may have been more adept at concealing their own sins and struggles. However, in the eyes of God, the putrid nature of their judgment was just as offensive as the outward odor that emanated from this family. Too often, those who come seeking Jesus have felt our judgment. Often, when someone shows up at our church, they are desperate. They are seeking a solution to whatever ailments they are experiencing.

Our judgment overshadows our love, and at least in that moment, they interpret our reaction to them as God's reaction.

2. Pride and Self-Righteousness:

On the flip side, some individuals may fall into the trap of pride and self-righteousness when they perceive themselves as more spiritually advanced than others. This can lead to a judgmental attitude and a lack of empathy for those who are still on their spiritual journey. Pride can be a significant barrier to humility and genuine spiritual growth for ourselves and others.

The situation involving the family served as a stark illustration of the dynamics unfolding within the church community. People began to engage in the perilous practice of spiritual comparison, and regrettably, this led to the emergence of pride and self-righteousness among certain members. It is vital to keep in mind that according to evangelical Christian theology, all sins are considered equal in the eyes of God, with the exception of blasphemy. While there may not be a universal theological consensus on the precise nature of this sin, many interpretations suggest that blasphemy against the Holy Spirit involves ignoring the Spirit's voice for an extended period, leading us to become conditioned to disregard its guidance in our lives. However, it is safe to conclude that no one within the church was guilty of blasphemy. Nevertheless, they were undeniably guilty of passing judgment and succumbing to the snare of spiritual pride.

Within the church, there was a woman who had recently transitioned from one of the larger churches in the community to attend our church plant. She came from a relatively affluent background, and as a church plant, individuals like her were invaluable not only for their financial support but also for their potential to become high-capacity leaders—a resource that many church plants are desperately seeking. She invited me to lunch one day, and after a little small talk, the subject of that family became a topic of conversation. She expressed concern that as long as "that family" was attending, we would have difficulty growing the church.

I couldn't deny the validity of her observation on the surface. My response, however, was rooted in the belief that while some struggles may be readily apparent, we all grapple with challenges, and as followers of God, we are called to exercise patience and compassion in our service to others. I won't go into further details about our conversation, but regrettably, it concluded with her deciding to leave the church. I must admit that her departure was painful, considering that we needed leaders and financial support. Nevertheless, I couldn't have continued leading the church if I had yielded to her suggestion that I should ask the struggling family to leave.

During our conversation, at one point, she exclaimed, "Pastor, I'm just not as good a Christian as you are." In response, I expressed my uncertainty about finding biblical support for the concept of varying degrees of Christianity. I believed that such notions were human inventions and rooted in spiritual pride.

3. Loss of Authenticity:

Constantly comparing oneself to others can lead to a loss of authenticity in one's faith. Some individuals may be tempted to mimic the practices or behaviors of others, even if they don't resonate with their true beliefs and convictions. This can result in a superficial spirituality that lacks depth and authenticity.

I was raised in a holiness denomination during the 1970s, where one prevailing interpretation of holiness and sanctification emphasized being "set apart." As a result, we often demonstrated our commitment to holiness and entire sanctification by abstaining from certain activities. These included refraining from dancing; many women chose not to cut their hair, wear makeup, engage in nail care, or adorn themselves with jewelry. As teenagers, we were restricted from wearing shorts, attending movies, or participating in mixed-gender swimming.

The challenge with this interpretation of being "set apart" based on dress and activities lies in its superficiality. It effectively constitutes a works-based theology, which contradicts the Bible's clear teaching that we are saved by grace through faith. True transformation, according to Scripture, originates from an inward change that radiates outward. While certain activities may be influenced by this inner transformation, they are not pursued for the sake of outward appearances. Instead, they stem from a deliberate choice to walk the path of life.

As previously mentioned, repentance signifies a change of direction, a turning away from a path of spiritual death toward one of life. When faith is reduced to mere outward observances, it can inadvertently foster hypocrisy and promote a "fake it till you make it" mindset. Such a faith lacks authenticity, and in a world where the next generation is seeking genuine and trustworthy leaders, any semblance of insincerity is easily discerned.

4. Jealousy and Resentment:

Spiritual comparison can breed jealousy and resentment towards those who appear to be experiencing more blessings, answered prayers, or spiritual growth. These negative emotions can poison relationships and hinder one's ability to genuinely rejoice with others in their spiritual journey.

Wow! This one resulted in the first murder. Cain killed Abel, his brother, in a fit of jealousy and anger.[173] The narrative goes like this: Cain and Abel were the sons of Adam and Eve, the first humans created by God. Both made offerings to God. Abel's offering, which was a lamb from his flock, was pleasing to God because it was offered with a willing and sincere heart. Cain's offering, on the other hand, consisted of the fruits of the ground, but it did not find favor with God.[174]

---

173. Genesis 4:1–16 (NIV)
174. Genesis 4:1–16 (NIV)

In response to God's acceptance of Abel's offering and rejection of his own, Cain became jealous and angry. God cautioned Cain that sin was crouching at the door, but he needed to master it. However, in his anger and jealousy, Cain lured Abel out into the field and killed him.[175]

Cain's act of murder was not only a result of jealousy but also a rejection of God's warning and an act of disobedience. This tragic event illustrates the consequences of harboring negative emotions and not dealing with them in a godly and constructive manner. It also highlights the destructive power of unchecked jealousy and anger. Perhaps you might think, "my jealousy and resentment would never cause me to hurt anyone physically. Remember Jesus' words from the very mountain he had just climbed.

> You have heard that it was said to those of old, 'You shall not murder; and whoever murders will be liable to judgment.' But I say to you that everyone who is angry with his brother will be liable to judgment; whoever insults his brother will be liable to the council; and whoever says, 'You fool!' will be liable to the hell of fire. [176]

5. Neglect of Personal Calling:

Each person's spiritual journey is unique, and God has a specific plan and calling for each individual. Comparing oneself to others can distract from God's unique path for one's life. It's essential to discern and embrace one's personal calling rather than trying to imitate someone else's.

I'm not suggesting that God has a predetermined path for each person. Instead, I'm referring to the concept of an ideal life, somewhat akin to how parents envision ideal futures for their children. We all bring unique experiences and gifts into our lives, and God uses these distinctive qualities to shape our life's journey and to extend His grace to the world through us.

---

175. Genesis 4:1–16 (NIV)
176. Matthew 5:21–22 (NIV)

For someone who chooses not to embark on a particular journey, like the climb we discussed, God's ideal plan for them may diverge from this specific path. It could be a matter of timing, or perhaps there's another significant event ahead that aligns better with their life's purpose. The full context of their situation and God's specific calling for their life remains a mystery to us. Fixating on their journey might divert our attention from our own.

Consider this: What if, in your pursuit of your own path, you missed the chance to engage in a meaningful conversation with someone whom God had intentionally placed in your life's journey because you were preoccupied with comparing yourself to those you've left behind? Such an oversight could lead to profound disappointment.

6. Impaired Relationships:

Spiritual comparison can negatively impact relationships within faith communities. When people compete or compare themselves with others, it can create divisions, jealousy, and an unhealthy atmosphere within the church or religious group.

7. Loss of Joy and Gratitude:

Constantly comparing one's blessings, experiences, or spiritual growth to others can rob individuals of the joy and gratitude they should feel for their unique journey and the blessings they have received from God.

A Path Up the Mountain

While these pitfalls may cause us to stall or stumble as we traverse the mountain, a path up the mountain can be found in developing a healthy perspective on one's spiritual journey. Here are some suggestions:

-   **Focus on Personal Growth**: Concentrate on your personal relationship with God and your individual spiritual growth rather than comparing yourself to others.

- **Practice Gratitude**: Cultivate a spirit of gratitude for the blessings and experiences God has granted you on your journey.
- **Seek Accountability**: Engage with a mentor or accountability partner who can provide guidance and encouragement without fostering unhealthy comparison.
- **Embrace Authenticity**: Be authentic in your faith journey, acknowledging your struggles and seeking growth in areas that matter to you and God.
- **Celebrate Others**: Celebrate the spiritual growth and blessings of others genuinely, without envy or comparison.
- **Pray for Humility**: Ask God to help you develop humility and a deep sense of your identity in Christ, which can guard against pride and insecurity.

Spiritual comparison is a common challenge, but it can hinder rather than enhance your faith journey. By focusing on personal growth, gratitude, authenticity, and humility, you can avoid the pitfalls of spiritual comparison and experience a more fulfilling and authentic relationship with God. We cannot lead someone to a place we have not been. This underscores the significance of authenticity as we mentor others on their faith journeys, emphasizing continual spiritual growth and fervently praying for God to unveil our own blind spots.

Keep Your Eyes on the Cross

This was not the only hill Jesus would climb in his ministry. He would traverse another hill called Golgotha at the end of his ministry, and this time, his climbing companions would be two thieves. This time, the huge crowds that gathered did not cheer him but jeered him. This time, they were not interested in abundant life; they just wanted Jesus dead. He had not met their expectations, and as often is the case today, so it was then the unforgivable sin!

I am reminded of a story that was circulated by a well-known evangelist in our community as a child. It is called *The Cross on the Church*:

> Once upon a time, on a dark and rainy evening, a little boy found himself sitting alone on the curb, weeping. He was lost and didn't know how to find his way home. Tears streamed down his face as he felt the weight of his predicament. A kind-hearted police officer happened to drive by and noticed the distraught child. Concerned for the boy's well-being, the officer pulled over, got out of his car, and approached the young boy.
>
> With a gentle and soothing voice, the officer asked the boy what was wrong. Through his sobs, the child explained that he had been playing with friends, but as time passed, he lost track of them, and now he couldn't find his way back home. The officer, filled with compassion, reassured the boy that he would help him.
>
> The officer began by asking if the boy knew his address, but the boy's tearful reply was, "No." Undeterred, the officer continued to inquire, asking if the boy recognized any landmarks or familiar places nearby that might lead them in the right direction.
>
> One by one, the officer suggested landmarks: the grocery store, the theater, the zoo. The boy shook his head at each suggestion, unable to recognize any of them. Desperation hung heavy in the air as the officer exhausted all possible options.
>
> Then, with a glimmer of hope in his eyes, the officer asked one last question, "Do you remember if there was a big cross on a church?" The little boy, still sniffling but now with newfound optimism, looked up and exclaimed, "Yes! Yes, I remember the cross!"
>
> In that moment, it was as if a ray of light had pierced through the darkness. The boy's faith was rekindled by the symbol of the cross in the church. He knew that if he could just get to the cross, he could find his way home.

With determination, the police officer, with the little boy in tow, followed the direction of the cross. And true to the boy's faith, they eventually arrived at the church. From there, the boy easily recognized the path leading to his home, and his tears turned into tears of relief and joy. His father and mother thanked the officer profusely, and that night, the little boy was hugged just a little tighter than he had ever been hugged before!

Keep your focus on the cross, and you will never go wrong. We cannot see the cross looking backwards on our journey. Looking back and focusing on those at the bottom of the mountain prevents you from being present with those who have made the climb with you and Jesus. Too much of our lives are spent looking backwards or forwards. Focus on the here and now.

The Key of a Consequential Faith Worth Pursuing

As I've written this book, I've wrestled with the task of crafting a guide to discipleship that is both easy to understand and pertinent while also acknowledging the inherent tension within the kingdom of God. It's a tension that's constantly unfolding, yet we can offer important keys to the next generation to help shape and unlock their faith through mentoring and discipleship.

One clear takeaway about the next generation and beyond is their pursuit of a faith that carries significance. When we fail to set realistic expectations for the faith climb, we risk betraying their trust. As much as the joy and freedom of being a companion of Jesus inspire us, we must also warn them of the dangers.

"Consider it pure joy, my brothers and sisters, whenever you face trials of many kinds, because you know that the testing of your faith produces perseverance. Let perseverance finish its work so that you may be mature and complete, not lacking anything."[177]

In the climb of faith, there will be physical challenges. Being a Christ follower doesn't guarantee immunity from sickness, including serious diseases like cancer and COVID-19. I recall when COVID-19 emerged, some Christians believed they would

---

177. James 1:2–4 (NIV)

be protected from illness, but some fell ill or even passed away. Within a few months, we were able to identify some co-morbidities that increased the likelihood of complications from COVID-19. However, it is wise to walk carefully when traversing new terrain. Diana, the thirty-five-year-old I mentioned in the previous chapter, was absolutely dedicated to the Lord and had unwavering faith—she still died. Following Jesus does not guarantee an easy climb. As we climb, encourage your companions to watch where they step and keep their footing sure. Scripture tells us many times not to fear, but it does not tell us we are immune from sickness or troubles.

There will be moments of fear and doubt. Some may criticize others for doubting, but faith doesn't eliminate fear and doubt. Faith is having the audacity to trust God despite those feelings, knowing that Jesus is with us on the climb. Face forward, lean into it, dig in your feet, grab the hand of a friend, and ask them to pull you up, then you reach down and take the hand of someone else.

In essence, what makes us Christians holy is that God dwells in our hearts. A glance at the Bible shows that being a Christian can intensify life's challenges. Be honest with your mentees as you invite them to join you on this climb. Share both victories and failures to offer hope during tough times.

Do not rush. In our fast-paced world, we often expect quick results. But mentoring and discipleship aren't like microwaving food; they're more like a slow-cooked meal. Microwaved food heats quickly, but it also cools quickly. A consequential faith needs a slow cooker to be sure it is "heated" throughout. Some of my most valuable lessons came from life's inconveniences that slowed me down. We can immerse them in scripture. We can teach them to pray, and introduce them to every spiritual discipline, from journaling to silence. But it is not going to speed up the formation of faith. Faith is formed in the crucible of the fires of experiences as we climb the mountain of faith with Jesus.

The disciples had three years with Jesus, and towards the end of His ministry, some of them were still arguing about who would be the greatest in the kingdom of God and asking to be on his "right and left" when he was lifted up. Jesus essentially replied, "You have no idea what you are asking."[178]

Do not project your experiences onto them. Everyone's journey is as unique as the person. There might be similarities, and where those similarities exist, offer guidance and wisdom. But your role is the guide. Be intentional about always pointing them back to Jesus. Remember, you do not have to be the expert.

Cultivate Wisdom

In today's fast-paced and information-saturated society, the next generation has unparalleled access to knowledge. However, the abundance of information can also lead to confusion and distraction. Help them distinguish between valuable wisdom and empty noise. Teach them to filter the messages they encounter, seeking that which is rooted in biblical truth and moral integrity. Knowledge is power, but true wisdom comes from knowing God.[179] Wisdom is not merely the accumulation of facts and information; it's the discernment to apply that knowledge in ways that honor God and serve others. It's about understanding the deeper truths of life, love, and purpose. As you mentor and guide the next generation, emphasize the importance of seeking divine wisdom in every aspect of their lives.

Encourage them to cultivate a heart of wisdom through prayer, meditation on God's Word, and seeking counsel from those who have walked the path of faith. Wisdom allows us to navigate the complexities of the world with grace, humility, and integrity. It helps us make choices that align with God's will and contribute positively to the lives of those around us.

---

178. Matthew 20:20–28 (NIV)
179. Proverbs 2:6 (NIV)

Likewise, share with them the importance of applying wisdom in their relationships, careers, and daily decisions. Let them understand that wisdom is not static but a lifelong pursuit. Just as a climber must constantly adapt to changing conditions on the mountain, so too must they adapt and grow in wisdom as they journey through life.

While the world may offer shortcuts and quick fixes, impress upon them that the enduring legacy of faith is built on the foundation of true wisdom. It's a legacy that doesn't waver with the shifting sands of culture or trends. As they climb the mountain of faith, let them grasp the hand of divine wisdom, allowing it to guide their steps and shape their character.

End of Chapter 7 Summary: Unlocking Consequential Faith

This is a call for us to be climbing companions with the next generation. It is a generation hungry for a faith that is not passive but active, transformative, and consequential. We must be there to guide, support, and love them unconditionally. As mentors and guides, we hold the torch of wisdom, illuminating their path to a faith that stands the test of time.

Disciple-making is a sacred journey of coming alongside a person as they grow in following Jesus in every area of their life. It is walking with a person as they process and change how they believe the world works, as their vision of what life could be and should be is transformed because of their commitment to follow Jesus and belong to the kingdom of God.

The journey ahead may be challenging and the terrain unpredictable, but together, as a community of faith, we can empower the next generation to reach new heights in their relationship with God and their impact on the world. The call is clear: will you be their climbing companion? Will you stand with them as they navigate the rocky slopes of life?

I hope you've found this book to be a thought-provoking journey into the depths of faith, and I genuinely hope you've enjoyed the exploration as much as I've enjoyed guiding you through it. As I mentioned in the preface, this book was never intended to be a straightforward "how-to" guide but rather a compass pointing you towards your prayer closet—the place where transformative encounters with God occur.

I have shared some keys to a consequential faith, but they're more descriptive than prescriptive. They're not a guaranteed formula for the next generation to have a meaningful relationship with the Lord. Some may not see the institutional church as essential. They may not see the local church as a means of nurturing their faith. Give them time.

The next generation wants to climb the mountain. They want the rope, the shoes, the gloves, helmets, and everything else that goes with the climb. They also want *you to join them on the climb.* Offer some guidance, but mostly just be there for them. Love them enough to hang out with them, even if their faith doesn't look exactly like yours, or agree with them politically. Even if they do not commit to going to your church. They want no-strings-attached relationships. They have had way too many transactional relationships. They want unconditional love.

This journey began during my extensive research while working on my dissertation. I embarked on that path with certain assumptions about the nature of a consequential faith, only to discover that some of my preconceived notions were, indeed, wrong. What had once been pessimism about the future generations transformed into a profound hope.

As I wrote this book, I revisited that research and found my hope reaffirmed. We may soon witness a transformational era in Christianity. Gen Z, often seen as the next generation, has the potential to shape the faith's future, just as their oldest predecessors, the greatest generation-built America.

But the path ahead is steep and challenging. They need companions, mentors, and guides to help them navigate the terrain and reach for Jesus' outstretched hand. Will you answer the call to be their climbing companions? Will you stand with them as they navigate life's rocky slopes? My hope is that this book has inspired you to embrace this role. Together, as a community of faith, we can empower the next generation to reach new heights in their relationship with God and their impact on the world.

Thank you for joining me on this journey. May your faith continue to grow as you extend a hand to help others ascend the mountain of faith. Remember, if the mountain were smooth, it would be almost impossible to climb.

Principles to Becoming Climbing Companions

Principle 1: Focus on the Cross

Just as the lost boy in the story found his way home by following the cross in the church, encourage others to keep their focus on the cross of Jesus. It's a symbol of faith and a source of guidance in challenging times. Together, fix your eyes on the cross as you journey forward.

Principle 2: Share Your Journey

Be open and honest about your own faith journey, including the challenges and doubts you've faced. Sharing both victories and failures can offer hope and encouragement to those you mentor. Remember that faith is formed through experiences as you climb the mountain of faith with Jesus.

Principle 3: Cultivate Wisdom

In a world filled with information, help the next generation distinguish between valuable wisdom and empty noise. Teach them to seek divine wisdom through prayer, meditation on God's Word, and seeking counsel from experienced believers. Wisdom will guide their steps and shape their character as they climb the mountain of faith.

As you embrace these ways of becoming climbing companions, you can empower the next generation to reach new heights in their relationship with God and their impact on the world.

A Prayer for Unlocking Consequential Faith in the Church of Tomorrow and Being a Climbing Companion

Lord,

Your brief journey on this earth serves as a powerful reminder that the journey of faith is not a passive endeavor. Just as You humbly left Your throne and descended into the challenges of this world, climbing mountains to teach and guide those who walked with You, we too must not remain spectators. We cannot merely stand at the mountain's base, encouraging the next generations to pursue a consequential faith. Instead, we must join them in the climb, side by side.

Grant us the wisdom we need as we ascend and help us keep our eyes fixed on the cross, the symbol of our faith and source of strength. Protect us from the comparison trap that can divert our focus and enable us to live fully in the present moment of the climb, one step at a time.

Lord, may our faith be authentic, always attributing our successes to Your grace and shaping the identity of those who journey with us. Remind us that even when we stumble, we need not start anew; instead, we secure our footing and continue the climb.

In Your name, we pray.

Amen.

Reachable Questions for Reflection

1. Reflect on individuals in your life who have embarked on their own spiritual journeys and left a lasting impact through their faith and love for others. How have these individuals influenced your own faith journey and the lives of those around them?

2. Share any personal experiences where you or someone you know faced physical challenges or health issues

while on their faith journey. How did faith play a role in navigating these challenges, and what lessons were learned from those experiences?

3. Consider the concept of "not rushing" in discipleship and mentoring. In a world that often seeks quick results, discuss the importance of a slow-cooked faith journey. Have you encountered situations where patience and perseverance in faith were essential?

4. Reflect on the disciples' journey with Jesus and their aspirations of greatness in the kingdom of God. How can you avoid projecting your own experiences onto those you mentor and guide? Discuss the importance of always pointing them back to Jesus.

5. Explore the distinction between knowledge and true wisdom in the context of faith. How does easy access to information in the digital age impact the pursuit of wisdom rooted in knowing God? Share your thoughts on this topic.

6. Discuss the desire of the next generation for an active and participatory faith journey. How can you support and guide them in their pursuit of a meaningful relationship with God, even if their approach differs from traditional norms?

7. Share your reflections on the transformational potential of the next generation, such as Gen Z, in shaping the future of Christianity. What challenges and opportunities do you foresee for them on their faith journey?

8. Consider the call to be "climbing companions" with the next generation in their spiritual ascent. How can you actively respond to this call and stand with them as they navigate life's challenges and seek to draw closer to God?

9. Can you relate to the comparison trap? If yes, how did/does it affect your overall spiritual journey?

Are you eager to guide your team in connecting with future generations? Consider acquiring the Small Group Companion Guide, now available on Amazon.com in Kindle format. Additionally, explore the 8-week video curriculum presented by Dr. Skinner, accessible at www.reachablebook.com/smallgroup. These resources are crafted to support your leadership journey in engaging with the next generations.

Rev. Jeffery D. Skinner (Ed.D)
CEO Missional Church Planting & Leadership Development
www.missionaleadershipcoaching.com

Ask about my Free Workshop

"5 steps to launch and grow a kingdom minded church with a multiplication mentality in less than 1 year in YOUR community."

The last resource you will need for church
planting & revitalization:

Revitalize To Plant:Reshaping The Established Church to Plant Churches

Listen now top 50 podcasts in religion

Missional Leadership Coaching

Missional Leadership Coaching is a non-profit that works with churches across the nation and equips church planters around the world to plant missional churches. If you would like to donate to the mission or schedule a call to discuss how Dr. Skinner might partner with your church or organization to help you build the church of the next generation by Loving, Mentoring, and Leading, visit missionalleadershipcoaching.com or scan the QR code below.

I also offer a complimentary training here.

Dr. Skinner hosts a weekly podcast entitled Echoes Through Eternity now in its third season. There, we embark on a mission to amplify the stories God is echoing across the world. Our podcast is a vibrant platform dedicated to missional leaders, inviting them to share their inspiring journeys. Join us as we delve into the realms of church planting, revitalization, leadership development, and more. Our vision is to inspire, engage, and encourage leaders worldwide to plant missional churches and embrace servant leadership. Tune in and be part of this transformative conversation.

Made in the USA
Columbia, SC
02 July 2024

fce019c8-69de-499d-bc9e-c2f1bcc70315R07